When my heart was grieved
  and my spirit embittered,
I was senseless and ignorant;
  I was a brute beast before you.
Yet I am always with you;
  you hold me by my right hand.
You guide me with your counsel,
  and afterward you will take me into glory.
Whom have I in heaven but you?
  And being with you, I desire nothing on earth.
My flesh and my heart may fail,
  but God is the strength of my heart
  and my portion forever.

Psalm 73:21-26 (NIV)

SANDY

A heart for God

LEIGHTON FORD
tells the moving story of his son

Centre for
Faith and Spirituality
Loughborough University

Inter–Varsity Press

INTER-VARSITY PRESS
38 De Montfort Street, Leicester LE1 7GP, England

©1985 by the Leighton Frederick Sandys Ford, Jr., Scholarship Memorial Fund and Kevin Graham Ford Trust

First published in Great Britain 1985

British Library Cataloguing in Publication Data

Ford, Leighton
    Sandy: a heart for God: the story of Sandy Ford.
    1. Heart——Diseases
    I. Title
    362.1'9612'00924   RC682

ISBN 0-85110-470-3

Typeset in the United States of America
Printed in Great Britain by Cox & Wyman Ltd, Reading

Inter-Varsity Press is the publishing division of the Universities and Colleges Christian Fellowship (formerly the Inter-Varsity Fellowship), a student movement linking Christian Unions in universities and colleges throughout the United Kingdom and the Republic of Ireland, and a member movement of the International Fellowship of Evangelical Students. For information about local and national activities write to UCCF, 38 De Montfort Street, Leicester LE1 7GP.

To Debbie Jean and Kevin
  who are always as important to us as Sandy
And to his friends
  who loved him in his life and us in his death.

1. *Running to Win*   11

2. *The Boy with No Yellow Light*   17

3. *An Open Heart*   27

4. *High-School Class*   39

5. *New School, New Love, New Mission*   53

6. *A Carolina Gentleman in Post-Christian France*   73

7. *The Salt of Granville West*   97

8. *The Dying Days of Summer*   109

9. *Questioning Faith*   119

10. *A Great Fall*   127

11. *"Be Good to My Boy"*   141

12. *Finishing the Race*   165

   Epilog   173

Preface

THIS IS THE STORY OF OUR SON. I WANTED TO WRITE ABOUT SANDY simply because I love him and want others to know him too. The writing has been painful, but it has also been healing. Even in losing our son, we have been blessed with something few parents have: the privilege of seeing his life whole from beginning to end.

I have also had a sense of mission. My hope is that Sandy's story will speak to other young men and women who love life, who struggle with growing up and who want to have a heart for God.

Do I think Sandy was special? Yes, I do. Not only in the sense that each of us is given by God a unique possibility which can be seized and shaped in a life of faith; but by the testimony of friends and the intuition of my own spirit, I recognize that God put in him extraordinary goodness, commitment, courage—and something more.

Sandy's book is a work of love by all our family—his mother, Jeanie, and our two other special children, Deb and Kevin. In tears and laughter together we have relived his life. Out of those family rememberings, the outline of his story took shape. When I was planning, taking notes and writing, Jeanie and I talked over everything together. She added many details, the shades of human interest that I would have overlooked. In fact, while the book bears my name, it is also her story of Sandy—*ours,* not just mine.

I have tried to draw from many sources—our family, his letters and ours, journals which he (unknown to us) was keeping at some key points in his life, and the letters, reminiscences and conversations which we had from or with his friends.

Among them I must mention two. Martha Vetter, his prayer

partner at Chapel Hill, urged us to write. I kept her letter in the front of my notebook and it often kept me steady. Susan Wheelon freely made available to us the detailed memoirs she kept during their freshman friendship.

Jim Sire and Andy Le Peau were my editorial encouragers. They believed that Sandy's story would be interesting and significant to a wider circle than his own friends and family. They also made a key decision in assigning a writer-editor, John D. (Jack) Stewart, to work with me.

Jack deserves special tribute. He not only took my manuscript to shape and refine it, but for weeks immersed himself in Sandy's story—reading, reflecting, talking with friends and acquaintances, uncovering stories, gaining perspective. In those few weeks Jack became part of Sandy's life. I told him when he took my manuscript to work it over, "Jack, I ask only two things. Treat him with love. Treat him with honesty." He did. And I say thanks.

When Jo Boynton typed the manuscript, she had a special stake too. She and Steve lost their own boy when he was young. When I wrote down some of my feelings after Sandy died, she urged me to write the story.

We have tried to be very accurate and to check our memories and impressions both with our written sources and with others who knew Sandy. In an instance or two we have let our imagination create his mood. In two or three instances only names have been changed to guard the privacy of individuals.

"A heart for God" is on the marker at Sandy's grave. More importantly, it is that "something more" which made him what he was, what he is and what we hope will be passed on to others in the telling of his story.

Leighton Ford
Charlotte, North Carolina
April 1985

1
RUNNING
TO
WIN

*I*N THE COOL OF THE EVENING, HE STOOD WAITING FOR THE hand-off, shivering as much from coiled anticipation as from the spring breeze. The Queen City Relays were the big meet of the year. Before the race Coach Prince had told his distance medley team that they had a chance to set a meet record. And Sandy's was the key assignment—the final mile lap.

Only vaguely he sensed the rising crescendo of cheers. It was the Myers Park track—his home high school—and he wanted to do well. Sandy had a heart burning to win.

Now he waited under the lights.

He knew Mom was watching. He wished Dad could be there.

Five hundred miles north, at Fort Campbell, Kentucky, I was

sitting on the platform in another stadium getting ready to preach to the military and their families.

I glanced at my watch. Eight o'clock. As I prepared my thoughts, my seventeen-year-old son was preparing to run.

A week before I had watched Sandy at the Metrolina Relays. In my mind's eye I could still see his slim, almost gaunt figure as he rounded the curve into the back stretch. With the fluid stride of the natural runner, arms swinging smoothly, rhythmically, he had pulled ahead. I had been on my feet with the others yelling, "Come on, Sandy. Come on." He won. Then he brought the Myers Park Mustangs distance medley relay team a first in that event. My heart had swelled.

Now he shuffled his feet, jogged a few yards. Stopped, bent and stretched. Withdrew inside himself to concentrate. He had run the mile enough times to know what was ahead. A mile all out was a long way. Lungs would burn and heave. Heart would pound. Legs would feel pain. But they were going to get that record. "I can do it," he said to himself fiercely, "I can do it. We are going to do it." In a few moments he would reach out for the baton. It would be up to him.

Jeanie was in the stands, but she didn't want to be there. Watching her son stretch and warm up, she too was proud. But her pride was undermined by a fear. With every stretch and lift of his strong thighs, she was seeing the pudgy, doughboy legs of an infant. When she saw his runner's body, lithe and almost totally muscular, she could not forget the recent memory of his body sweating but cold to the touch, and his heart pounding at a fearsome rate, far beyond normal.

As his teammate drew near, Sandy saw that his team already had a clear lead. He moved onto the cinder track, waiting, grasping the baton—and then he took off.

What was Coach Prince yelling? He couldn't quite get it. Words of encouragement, he guessed. But the coach was actually trying to tell Sandy that they were behind time, with no chance for a record. But Sandy didn't know. And he was out for the record.

It wasn't easy to gauge times with no other runners pressing him. Relying on his inner clock, he went as fast as he dared, holding something back, maintaining the lead. Then, nearing the homestretch he knew it was time to pour it on, pour it on, pour it on, give it all he had.

As he rounded the last turn, the crowd was on its feet, yelling in a great din of encouragement.

"He's got a forty-yard lead," someone yelled.

"Maybe it will be a record," another answered.

Then, about twenty yards from the finish his legs suddenly wobbled. He managed to weave a few more yards, staggered and fell to the track. Gasping for breath, he groped for the dropped baton, rose, staggered forward and fell again just short of the finish line.

The crowd watched, stunned and silent. Glancing over his shoulder, seeing the second-place runner close, somehow he got on his hands and knees, grabbed the baton, half-stumbled and half-crawled the remaining ten yards, threw himself over the finish line and collapsed on the track. He had won.

In the stands Jeanie stood, numb with shock. Her mind stuttered with thoughts it did not want to think. She ran down from the stands.

Sandy was carried from the track to the infield, his heart fluttering rapidly in his chest, and was laid on the foam mattress of the high-jump pit. A small group gathered around. He threw up and was embarrassed. His girlfriend was there.

"My mom's in the stands," he said. "She'll be worried."

Stepping to where he could see her, Jeanie said, "Buddy, I'm here. Are you okay?" Was it the quiche lorraine she had fed him for supper that made him sick? Was this her fault?

His heart continued to flutter for another seven to eight minutes before it returned to a normal beat. He didn't run his other scheduled event.

Before he left the field Sandy talked with a reporter and told him that a few years ago he had had heart surgery to correct a problem that had caused a rapid and life-threatening arrhythmia. But the doctor had given him a hundred-per-cent clean bill of health. "He told me it wouldn't hurt to run and it hasn't bothered me until now. I've pushed myself before—real hard. I'm just not sure about the future right now. I'm gonna have to wait and see what the doctor says."

The next day I learned of Sandy's fall and finish. When I got home I read the stories both local papers carried on their sports pages. "Prep Runner Puts His Heart on the Line," said one headline, with a photo of Sandy sprawled on the track. The story described "what will be remembered as one of the most dramatic events ever in local sports."

To Jeanie, however, it wasn't dramatic; it was sheer trauma.

"I was proud of Sandy's running," Jeanie says now, "But I dreaded it, too.

"Sandy really wanted to continue his running in college. And his times were good enough. Several college coaches were interested in recruiting him. The fall he was a senior [1978] he had several heart flutters during cross-country. He finally gave in and agreed reluctantly with the doctor's new decision that he shouldn't run competitively anymore. He never did again. What the doctors didn't know was that anything Sandy did was competitive. He was so highly motivated. He always had to better his own time."

Looking back, I don't think Sandy should have been running at all. Earlier the doctors had said his heart could begin to flutter anytime—waking, sleeping, exercising or at rest. But I question whether we should have allowed him to go back to such a demanding sport. Sandy wanted to run and I wanted him to run. But Jeanie hated it. Jeanie and I could hardly talk about it for several weeks after he collapsed at the Queen City Relays. The issue produced tremendous tension between us, one of the few crises in our marriage.

So Sandy sat out spring track in his senior year. It was a hard decision, but the right one. And not for physical reasons only. When he shared with me his disappointment about track, I tried to get him to see that when God allowed one door to close, he would certainly open another. Perhaps a college career in sports would have consumed so much time that Sandy would not be able to give leadership in other areas. At first he resisted that idea. But he was already involved in high-school student government. He was beginning to sense that other things were important. But neither he nor I knew at that time just how much his leadership would mature and what impact it would have when he got to the University of North Carolina (UNC), Chapel Hill.

All the heart and drive that carried him across that Myers Park finish line in April 1978 would be poured into his relationship with God, his care for others, into everything he did. He was developing another kind of heart—a heart for God.

2
THE BOY
WITH NO
YELLOW LIGHT

H E WAS BORN IN A HURRY. HE PUSHED OUT OF JEANIE'S WOMB just minutes after she arrived at Presbyterian Hospital in the fall of 1960. And he lived as he was born, with terrific intensity.

Holding tightly to Jeanie's hand on a hot, clear August day, he walked to his first day of school. As they walked up the half-dozen steps into the school, he looked into her face and said, "Mom, I'll make *A*'s every day of my life." And he almost did. He always had a new goal, a new activity, a new standard to reach.

Once when he was little we were at the Fairmeadows Swimming Club, and I told him to put his head under the water. Uncertain and puzzled, both wanting and not wanting to do it, he put his hand on top of his head and tried to push himself under.

He seldom stood still. But it was eagerness, not hyperactivity. I can still see him the first year he played basketball at the YMCA. As the other little boys stood still waiting for the attempt at a foul shot, Sandy jumped and bounced—nonstop.

There was no coasting, no getting by, no medium range with Sandy. It was all out or full stop. He was impulsive, and I used to get impatient with him. "Pal, you have no yellow light! Take it easy!"

He loved sports. He loved to watch, and he loved to play. And he played them all—basketball, baseball, tennis, football, swimming, track. His natural athletic ability was good, but not outstanding. He was sturdy, but not particularly tall (just six feet) or particularly strong. That always bothered him because like most boys, he wanted more muscle. But he was quick, with great reflexes and good eye-hand coordination. What helped him most was his joy, his commitment and his enthusiasm. One of his friends marveled, "He never quit. He gave two hundred per cent in everything." He would throw up after little league football workouts; there was a scar on his elbow from an injury that never healed properly because he refused to sit out football until it got better.

He gave everything he had to everything he did. And he tried many things: woodworking, collections of whatever, rock polishing. Each activity, at the time, was "most important." Sometimes he drove us a little crazy. The rattle of his rock-polishing set went on twenty-four hours a day for weeks, until his sister Debbie threatened to throw it and him out.

His intensity seemed to make him accident prone. He got hit by a bat and needed stitches, pulled the bird bath over on his head, caught his finger in a swing hinge and almost cut it off, and got bit by a big dog in the neighborhood.

Achieving was so important to him it caused problems. As an athlete he tried too hard and seldom relaxed enough to really do his best. Old family movies always showed Sandy with a frown on his face from concentrating. When he won, he was elated; but when he lost, you could not live with him. He was never able to live up to what he thought he should be able to do. We dreaded his losing a basketball game on Saturday morning because it would spoil the rest of the weekend.

Where did Sandy's extraordinary drive and intensity come from? Was he trying too hard to please me? Many times I remember standing at the edge of the basketball court or football field. After he had made a good shot or tackle, he would look over to see if Jeanie and I were watching. We always let him know how pleased we were.

Yet while he always sought our approval, it was hard for him to receive it. When he was a baby, I would give him a bottle in the middle of the night and try to cuddle him. But he would stiffen and push off. Something kept him a little separate. Many times after a success or a failure, I would hug him and let him know how much I loved him. But it was not easy for him to take. His impossibly high expectations of himself were often irritating. While he always cooperated with his coaches, he found it very difficult to take instructions or suggestions from me or anyone in the family. He was so hard on himself. But why did he have such difficulty receiving love or help?

There was so much of me in Sandy, and so much of Sandy in me. Is that what drew us close and yet kept him a bit apart? Was it too important for him to be me—or to be like me—or to be what he thought I was? Was I so good and perfect in his eyes that he could never let himself just be Sandy?

After all my musings, I still can't explain him. I am always left with something irreducible, innate, something not to be explained by Jeanie's or my influence for good or ill. His intensity was inborn, as if he sensed that he had to live life fully because some inner clock knew God had wound him up for just twenty-one years.

He was late speaking his first words. When he finally, ponderously began putting words together, the sentences seemed to go round and round. Debbie, our oldest, was good with words, and Sandy may have been a little intimidated by his talkative family. We even wondered if he needed speech therapy, but found that he had no trouble at all in school.

Still he was precocious about spiritual things. When he was small we had four or five kittens. One day he took them all into the bathroom and baptized each one in the toilet.

A scrupulous sense of fairness and honesty was born in him too. We sometimes thought he had an overly sensitive conscience. Once at an Atlanta Falcon's game, we saw a man bribe a gate attendant for a place in a restricted parking area. That almost spoiled the whole day for Sandy. Better that than indifference to morals.

Our housekeeper, Sally Wade, also recalls how committed he was to fairness and justice. "I remember one time it rained real bad and my car got stuck in a bog on the side of the road next to your house. I couldn't get the car out of that bog, no way. Sandy came out to see could he help me. Sandy wasn't old enough to drive, but he knew how to drive. I said, 'Sandy, get in there. See can you get it out.' But he couldn't either. So he got a man from the filling station to get a wrecker, and the man pulled me out. I asked the man how much it would cost. He said, 'Eight dollars.' So I paid and he left. Sandy said, 'I'm going to make mother give you back your money, 'cause it wasn't your fault you got stuck.' I don't know what he told her, but that Friday when she started to pay me, she called Sandy downstairs and said, 'See, I'm paying Sally and I'm giving her the money back she paid the man.' And he said, 'Well, it's only right, Mother.' He went back upstairs and

I was tickled to death."

He could be a Pharisee of the Pharisees when it came to rules. One day when I was in my study, I overheard him and Deb playing one-on-one basketball in the drive. She wanted to play heedless of rules; he insisted otherwise. What bothered me most was that their disagreement made it impossible for them to play at all.

He was full of fun and mischief as well. We still laugh about how his kindergarten teacher called to say that Sandy had climbed a tree and from that lofty perch was going potty on the scene below. He fought with Deb and Kevin, as most children do with their brothers and sisters; they were a headache to travel with; they ruined the locks on all the upstairs rooms, chasing each other, slamming doors and then trying to pick the locks— with scissors!

Many have told Jeanie and me that Sandy was stricter and more conservative than we were. He was never inclined to rebel, as were Deb and Kevin. Even in high school he was always in by eleven by his own volition. If he had gone astray, he probably would have gone the way of the elder brother in Jesus' parable of the prodigal son. The younger brother ran away with his share of his father's fortune and led a wild and profligate life. The older brother was the "good guy." He never left home, was always dutiful, available and obedient. But the elder brother was just as far from his father as was the younger son, even though he never strayed a foot from the family farm.

All this is not to say that we did not have our differences about what he could and could not do. Nor do I mean that he did not face the temptations that all young people do. He did. I believe that it was the grace of God in his life that took his goodness and made it far more winsome than self-righteous.

His strong desire to be and to do right could and did, at times, make him difficult, starchy and unbending. But as Sandy internalized this uprightness he also learned to feel and show affection and companionship for those of his peers who were far less demanding of themselves. Sometimes righteousness by itself can be cold and forbidding. But it was goodness joined to acceptance and understanding that made Sandy attractive.

Wilma Miller, one of the teachers at Alexander Graham Junior High, later wrote, "I never had an opportunity to teach Sandy, but it was impossible not to be aware of his tremendous influence. . . . He set such a fine example for his peers because of his high moral and intellectual standards, and yet the things his friends have mentioned most often have been his friendliness and genuine 'caring.' "

Sandy had a great need to understand the gospel of grace, for himself and others. He needed to see that being a Christian is not primarily an achievement, but rather a gift. And that came as he grew.

When he was six years old, he was lying on the red carpet in our den watching one of his Uncle Billy's crusade services on television. Billy Graham was talking that night about the Ten Commandments, how it was impossible for any of us to keep them in spirit as well as in the letter. And I am sure he explained, as he always does, what the gospel is—that all of us have sinned, that none of us is good enough to be acceptable to God, and that Jesus by his perfect life and his perfect death made it possible for us to be accepted if we would trust him. Then came the invitation. Sandy was lying on his stomach with his head propped up in his hands as he watched the people walk forward. He turned to Jeanie and said, "Mom, do I have to be there to do that?" We explained that he did not. That night he acknowledged his need and asked Jesus to come into his life and to be his Savior.

Before this we had prepared the hearth of his heart for the fire of the Spirit by praying for him and with him, reading the Bible to him and Deb or by having them act out the parts of Daniel and the lions and the other Bible stories in our family devotions. We had prayed that he would come to know the Lord.

Those were happy years for us. Although I was often away, we had great times together when I was home. My family has always meant a lot to me. My natural mother gave me up for adoption when I was born. My adopted parents were already middle-aged when they took me in and, by my teen-age years, my adopted mother had become emotionally ill and she and my dad fought much of the time. Although they took in some foster children from time to time, I had no brother or sister that I was close to. So, although I had many friends, my early years were often lonely. Consequently, the family Jeanie and I made together was important to me. Jeanie was a lonely child too, as her nearest sibling was eight years older. When we met at Wheaton, we were just delighted to have each other, to share love. And we are still deeply in love.

When the children came, we both poured our lives into them. I loved to play basketball and throw football and baseball with the boys. We played indoor games too. Sometimes I would take Sandy out of school a bit early in the afternoon, and we would go together to watch an exciting movie matinee. For a couple of years we watched every episode of "Combat" on television, with Sandy sitting in my lap.

Almost every night when I was home, from the time he was six until he was in his late teens, I would reserve bedtime for him, tell him a story and pray with him. One series of stories about a boy and his horse lasted for years.

Summer vacations were always special too. We enjoyed the beautiful South Carolina beaches, but we loved the North Carolina mountains. Julian and Joanne LeCraw, good friends of ours from Atlanta, had a mountain home in the little western North Carolina town of Highlands. Every summer for about ten years they invited us to use it for a week or two. How we enjoyed our family and friends! There was a pond fed by cold mountain water, and at least once every vacation we had a contest to see who could stay in longest. Sandy or I usually won.

Another favorite vacation spot was Lost Valley Ranch in Deckers, Colorado, run by Bob and Marian Foster. There one summer we met and found instant rapport with Bill and Ellie Dooner and their family. Bill was of Irish Catholic background. Ellie was from good German Mennonite stock. At fourteen, Sandy was hopelessly attracted to Julie, their oldest daughter. She became his first special girl.

The Christmas after we met them, the Dooners invited Sandy to go to Florida with them on a midwinter vacation. When he went down his hair was straight and when he came back it was kinky—as if he had had a permanent. But it never straightened out. Whether it was the Florida humidity or his passion for Julie, we never quite figured out. But we never let Sandy forget Julie had "made his hair curl."

When Bill and Ellie moved to Ireland for several years, they invited Sandy to visit them. Those summer weeks of 1975 were exciting. He fell in love with Ireland's lush green hills. The Dooners are as loose in their schedule as we are firm in ours, and it was broadening for Sandy to be taken in as part of their relaxed and carefree atmosphere. He came back home laughing and full of stories of shelling mountains of green peas that grandmother Yordy had picked and riding horses at full speed on the rolling plains by the Irish seaside. He affected them too. Julie later told me that Sandy was one of the strongest influences for Christ she had ever known. "He never wavered," she said, "and yet he was so much fun."

As school started that year Sandy was full of anticipation and boyish good spirits. On the first Saturday in September he sat in the privacy of his room and made a tape to send to Julie in

Ireland. In the high unchanged voice of early adolescence he told Julie all he was doing. Geometry he thought would be "pretty much fun." Social studies would be one of his hardest subjects. He really liked industrial arts and was going to make an oval-shaped coffee table (which won first place in a statewide contest and is still a prized possession in our den). When he came home from school, he told Julie, he liked to just sit and relax and play tennis or perhaps go bike riding after finishing his homework. Just the week before, he and his friend Donny Little had ridden about fifty miles out to the airport and down to the South Carolina border, stopping at the Pizza Hut. At church he had just been moved up to the senior high group. It was "pretty fun" to be with the older kids. He laughed about a joke I had played on Mom. A couple of nights before, I had come home from London on an earlier flight than I had planned. When I got home, I called Jeanie from the downstairs phone to her phone up in the bedroom and told her I was in London. He laughed and laughed at the look on Jeanie's face when I went upstairs to greet her a few seconds later.

Then he ended the tape. "Pretty soon I will be starting basketball practice. I will be working on that for a long time. I hope to make the varsity team at AG [Alexander Graham]. Even though I don't get to play much I want to make it for the experience. I really hope to have a good year at school this year. I know it will be a lot of fun because I am older. I keep looking back at the good times we had and the fun it was." Then he stopped and looked at his calendar. "Today is Saturday the 6th. I just checked."

That tape marked the end of a blissful, idyllic summer and the end of Sandy's boyhood days of ease and innocence. What followed was the beginning of the end of Sandy the puritan, the beginning of Sandy the gracious man of God and the beginning of the end.

On October 7, one month after Sandy made that tape, I was at a conference of Methodist pastors meeting at the Thomas Watson estate in upstate New York. I had been invited to speak. We had just arrived and were eating supper when I was given a message that my secretary was on the phone. Leola's voice was tense, but it was obvious that she was trying to be calm. "Leighton, don't be worried. Sandy is in the hospital. They say there is some problem with his heart. But we think he is going to be all right."

A problem with his heart? My son, Sandy? The athlete with no yellow light? What could possibly be wrong with the heart of a fourteen-year-old boy? My mind was a chaos of questions.

3
AN
OPEN
HEART

*M*INUTES LATER I WAS ON THE PHONE TO JEANIE AT MEMORIAL Hospital in Charlotte. I knew how to interpret the tremble in her voice, and it scared me. Sandy had called late that afternoon from school, saying he didn't feel well, something was wrong with him, could she come and pick him up? When she arrived, he was sitting with his back against the building. He waved her to come to him. But Jeanie, who had been lying down not feeling well herself when Sandy called, signaled him to come to the car. As he crossed the lot, she could see from the way he carried himself that something was very wrong. When he got in, she saw that he was unusually pale, sweating profusely, and his heart was visibly pounding in his chest. Yet he was cold to the touch.

Jeanie rushed him to a pediatrician friend, Blair Bryan. When

Blair checked Sandy's pulse—it was over three hundred per minute—he immediately put Sandy in the back seat, got in with him, keeping one hand on his heart and the other on his pulse, and ordered Jeanie to drive them to Memorial Hospital.

While we were on the phone, Sandy was in the emergency room, his pulse still racing over three hundred. They were trying a series of drugs to halt the arrhythmia. He was young and strong, and had no history of heart problems, but no heart could bear that pace indefinitely.

The next two hours were a blurred montage of phone calls to the hospital—worse news each time—and attempts to arrange an emergency flight to Charlotte. There were no scheduled flights that time of day. Sandy's heart had not slowed down; he asked Jeanie, "Mom, am I going to be O.K.?" With her own heart and voice breaking, she reassured him. But she had no assurance of her own.

At last I arranged to divert a chartered plane to Charlotte. When I phoned Jeanie to tell her, she came on the line with good news. "Darling, he's all right. Blair just came from emergency with a big smile and thumbs up. Sandy's heart has converted to a normal pace. Blair says it's one part medicine, nine parts prayer." On the plane, I collapsed into my seat with exhausted relief and thanksgiving. I had been dreading getting off in Charlotte only to find that my son had died. Now, thank God, he was all right.

Sandy was suffering from a problem called Wolfe-Parkinson-White syndrome (WPW). The normal heart is equipped with pathways along which electrical impulses travel to make the heart beat. These impulses are governed and made regular by what is called the A-V node. People with WPW are born with surplus electrical circuitry—one or more extra pathways which by-pass the A-V node. Sandy had two extra pathways. The condition was not all that rare, but in Sandy's case, these accessory pathways conducted at an abnormally fast, life-threatening rate. This is why his heart had been racing at up to three hundred sixty beats per minute.

This superfast arrhythmia could happen any time, we were told, but something had to trigger it, something had to open the gate to allow the normal electrical impulses to pass along the unregulated accessory pathways. What was this trigger? Sandy, true to form, had stayed after basketball practice that day to practice more on his own. It was after a drink of cold water that the arrhythmia began. Was it the hard exercise or the cold water? Was it a freak, one-time thing or would it happen again? The doctors at Memorial in Charlotte did not know.

After the initial scare, Sandy's response was natural, predictable: "I want to get out of here." But when the doctors told him that this was a serious condition and that he might have to be on medication for a long time, perhaps for the rest of his life, he rebelled. "Why do I have to have something wrong with me? I don't want to be a freak! Why should I have to take medicine for the rest of my life?" To this young athlete, the prospect of some impairment to his heart and activity was unbearable. He had no perspective, of course: what was life without basketball, running? He could not see what a relatively minor thing a pill or two a day was.

I called all over the country to learn about WPW. I discovered that the most advanced research on this problem was being done at Duke University Medical Center, Durham, North Carolina— only three hours away! In fact, through the work of Dr. John Gallagher, an electrophysiological cardiologist, Duke had become the world center for WPW research. We sent him Sandy's records from Memorial Hospital. What he saw so alarmed him that he called us immediately. Sandy's was not the ordinary case of WPW. Because he had conducted at such a fast rate, another unexpected attack could prove fatal. He urged us to bring Sandy to Duke for further tests and rearranged his schedule to admit him in the next few days.

The drive from Charlotte to Durham is beautiful. The highway undulates through almost unbroken oak and pine forest, accented with dogwood. But we were too preoccupied to appreciate it. Sandy was particularly cut off, even more silent and uncommunicative than usual. His eyes stared ahead, focused on nothing in the visible world, probing, I guessed, the unseen world of life's questions and answers: This development did not accord with the rules; the game was not supposed to be played this way. If you trained hard and played fair, you were supposed to win—or at least lose with honor and return to try again. What he anticipated at Durham, I do not know. He never said. But it must have looked to him like retirement before his career had even begun.

I'm glad we did not know what was in store. We expected to stay only a couple of days, but it would be three weeks before we returned home. And Sandy would pass both his fifteenth birthday and the most severe trial of his life and ours.

Dr. John Gallagher is an Irish Catholic New Yorker who was transplanted to the South during his medical training. Like many outstanding scientists, he is initially shy, almost timid, but utterly confident and a superb communicator in his field. He was pioneering research in WPW. Every problem was a challenge, every successful case a personal triumph. He had assembled an expert team in a field that is still relatively new—mapping the electrical patterns of the heart. They had to determine first whether any drug or combination of drugs would alter the electrical patterns of Sandy's heart. The problem might be handled with medication. They would also attempt to map these electrical patterns in order to determine as precisely as possible the location of the extra electrical conduits. This knowledge would be indispensable if surgery were necessary.

The most difficult tests were those in the cath lab where Sandy had to lie still on a hard table for up to eight hours a day with three catheters inserted in veins—one in his leg, one in his arm and one in his groin. He endured this without a murmur. The team recorded thousands of pages of tracings indicating the effect of the drugs. These had to be carefully analyzed.

As the hours turned into days and weeks, and the brightness of October gave way to the bleakness of early November, our hopes for an easy solution waned. One by one the options of treatment by medication were eliminated. As if we were traveling through a canyon that grew narrower and narrower, the walls pressed in on us. Only gradually did we realize how serious the situation was.

Sandy was as patient and cooperative as a fourteen-year-old could be. But one night, after an inexperienced nurse's aide jabbed him repeatedly in an unsuccessful attempt to draw blood, we heard him yelling far down the hall, telling her to stop and get someone who knew what she was doing. She wrote on his chart, "Patient refused to give blood."

Late on a Friday night, Dr. Gallagher met with us to sum up the testing. He brought along a model of a heart to show us the location and nature of Sandy's problem. He took time to explain and to answer our questions. He never talked down to us or to Sandy and seemed to appreciate particularly Sandy's comprehension of the problem. He explained to us that none of the then available medications would in his judgment guarantee a safe passage for Sandy outside the hospital. His clear and unequivocal recommendation was for surgery—as soon as possible. He had already tentatively reserved the next Monday morning. Dr. Will Sealy, one of the leading thoracic and heart surgeons in the country who often worked with Dr. Gallagher, would be available to do the surgery. Although the surgery to correct WPW was relatively new—Sandy would be only the forty-seventh case they had done at Duke—and although Sandy's pathway was located in one of the more difficult areas at the back of the heart, still John was relatively confident they could correct the problem. There were, of course, no guarantees.

That night our son grew up before our eyes. He listened attentively to John Gallagher. He asked intelligent questions about the drugs, the electrical pathways and patterns, what set off the erratic beat that opened the gate to the extra conduits, what were the chances of successful surgery and the consequences if it were not successful? He probed about how restricted his activities would be afterward. Particularly he wondered if he would be able to return to sports.

After the doctor left the room, he cried. He asked why this was happening to him. Then thoughtfully and seriously he made the decision that if we felt it was best, he was prepared to go ahead with the surgery. We had never seen him in such a crucible before, and it made visible depths of character we had never seen.

But John Gallagher saw things we had not. "The first time I saw Sandy," he said much later, "I thought of the Trappist monks at St. Joseph's Abbey in Spenser, Massachusetts. From across the abbey grounds we watched them come to services, the only time they used their voices. Silhouetted against the morning sun, just beyond an iron fence, they'd file by, close enough to touch. Their cowls shielded part of their faces, but you could see that they looked alive, resigned, pleasant. They wore this peaceful, purposeful smile. We used to joke about them being rejected gay personalities. But we always returned because you felt refreshed by them and the place. I remember thinking, 'You tell me they talk to Somebody? I believe it. Look at them. They know something or somebody the rest of us don't.' That's what I thought the first time I saw Sandy, and every time after. It wasn't what he said, but his attitude, his face—confident, comfortable, resigned."

That was part of Sandy. Perhaps it was harder on us than on

Sandy because we knew that a young boy's insecurity was still a part of him. One afternoon when he was eight I drove Sandy home from a piano lesson. Like Deb and Kevin, he loved music. But he never mastered an instrument as they did. On this day he was discouraged. He was not doing well in piano. (Shortly afterward, he gave up piano lessons—one of the few things he did not follow through on.) Worse yet, he had been in a touch football game with his friends down the street and he had not done well or as well as he thought he should.

"Every pass that was thrown to me I dropped," he moaned. And then feeling sorry for himself he said, "Dad, none of the guys like me."

I tried to argue him out of his self-pity, but he was not to be moved.

"Nope," he said. "No one loves me."

"But I love you," I protested.

"Nope," he said.

"Your mother loves you," I said. But he could not accept that either.

"Your sister loves you," I said. But he knew that wasn't true!

Finally, trying to get through all the resistance he was throwing at me, I said, "Well, Sandy, you know that God loves you."

That stumped him. He knew, of course, that the Bible said that. So he knew that he should believe it, especially when his daddy was a preacher and said so. Still he hesitated and said, "I'm not so sure."

Then I came up with what I was sure would convince him. "Sandy," I said, "God loved you so much that he sent Jesus to die for you."

There was a long silence. Then a sad eight-year-old voice said, "Dad, I think if God had known me, he never would've sent Jesus." That insecurity was still as much a part of Sandy as the mystical spirituality that John Gallagher saw.

Sandy was to learn some new things while at Duke University Medical Center. But he was not alone. Sunday afternoon, the day before his surgery, I walked into an empty hospital room across the corridor and stared out at the overcast November sky, the bare trees, the gray stone of the Duke buildings. Inside I was torn up. I felt as Abraham must have felt when the Lord asked him to lay his beloved son Isaac on an altar of sacrifice to see if Abraham was willing to trust God completely. *God, you were Sandy's father before I was. He belonged to you before he belonged to me. As you gave him to me, I give him back to you!* That night, as Deb and Jeanie slept in our Hilton motel room, I knelt to pray and found comfort in these words from Hosea 6:1-3 (LB).

"Come, let us return to the Lord; it is he who has torn us— he will heal us; He has wounded—he will bind us up. In just a couple of days, or three at the most, he will set us on our feet again, to live in his kindness! Oh, that we might know the Lord! Let us press on to know him, and he will respond to us as surely as the coming of dawn or the rain of early spring."

With these words and our confidence in Drs. Gallagher and Sealy, Jeanie and I rose the next morning and hurried to the hospital to see Sandy off to surgery. The percentages for a successful surgery were high. But Sandy was our son, not a statistic. And this was the first major trauma our family had been through.

Sandy was in bed but awake. He had already been given a shot to relax him. He was calm and peaceful. There was little to say. When they came for him, Jeanie and I went to the waiting room. During those long hours, we were thankful that friends were up at 4:00 A.M. at Campus Crusade for Christ headquarters in California to pray. People at "The 700 Club" were praying on the East Coast. Sandy's Uncle Billy was praying in Hong Kong. Julie Spivey, a Christian nurse assigned to Sandy, kept us informed and encouraged during the operation.

Gallagher and Sealy knew that Sandy had two extra pathways,

but they thought only one was dangerous. But that extra pathway which they intended to cut was very close to the normal pathway, the central conductive system of the heart. To cut that central system would make a pacemaker necessary, yet none of these pathways are visible. Dr. Sealy would have to estimate where the extra pathway was by his knowledge of the anatomy and from Gallagher's electrical mappings of Sandy's heart.

Once Sandy's chest was open, Dr. Sealy cut where he thought the extra pathway was. Then they paced the heart electrically to see if that pathway was still conducting. It was. He cut more. Again, they tested. Again he cut. Finally, the pathway would not conduct. It had been severed. The transition from the heart-lung by-pass machine to Sandy's heart was effected without a hitch.

While all this was going on, we waited. At last John Gallagher walked in with an Irish smile. The surgery had been successful. It was a personal as well as professional victory for John, for during the days of testing he had become attached to Sandy. He savored his success, and so, thankfully, did we. John looked up. "We had extra help in there today."

Before the operation, he had told Jeanie that after every successful operation they celebrated in the operating room with a cake.

"Did you have a cake?" she asked.

"No, we didn't. Not today."

That made Jeanie wonder if the doctors really felt the operation was a success.

Sandy's recovery was swift but painful. He was stuck all over with tubes and needles and swathed in bandages. Unable to talk at first, his eyes asked, "How did it go?"

Jeanie smiled, "They got your problem, Sandy."

In order to keep his lungs free of fluid, he had to cough; but this was extremely painful. Still, after weeks of bad news, we were relieved to know that he was going to be fine and could return to a normal life. He was out of acute care by the second day after surgery. After four days, the nurses gave him a fifteenth birthday party. And the next day, at Dr. Sealy's invitation, he watched an open-heart surgery.

The Sunday before Thanksgiving, seven weeks after his attack, I drove Sandy home. Deb and Kevin had a big sign reading "Welcome Home, Sandy!" at the end of the drive. And his church youth group was there with a golden retriever puppy for his birthday. Sandy immediately named him Czar since golden retrievers are Russian-bred dogs.

Delighted to learn that the doctors had forbidden him to mow the lawn or lift anything heavy for six months, Sandy was kept busy in those first weeks back home with many visitors. Guys came to talk. Girls brought him cookies.

At the suggestion of one of his teachers, Sandy wrote about his experience in an article he called "The Day My Heart Ran Away."

What does a fifteen-year-old kid do when he has to face the awesome reality of open-heart surgery? I never thought I could endure such a thing.

God came to me at a time when I needed him more than ever before. I had been brought up in a Christian home and had known Jesus Christ since I was six, but I remember so well that Friday night at Duke when I cried by my bedside with my parents to the Lord in my hour of need.

Prayer was one reality which God showed me and still shows me. Along with the encouragement from my parents, my brother and sister, Christians all over the world prayed for me. . . . Thousands of individuals whom I had never met had a concern for me.

Hosea 6:1 meant a great deal to me: "Come, let us return to the LORD; it is he that has torn us—he will heal us. He has wounded—he will bind us up." God used this situation to show himself to me and to show me my need to rely upon him.

God allowed Sandy's heart to run away to draw his spiritual heart closer to the Lord. Sandy found God's gift of grace in the grace of those who demonstrated their concern for him in prayer and friendship. This was crucial for a young man who struggled sometimes with insecurity and inferiority and who still carried inside him that eight-year-old's fear that if God really knew him, he would not have sent Jesus.

We watched as he changed. Friendships deepened. He became more gracious. He had begun to learn that his worth, and everyone's, is not an achievement, but a gift, a grace from God. He always referred to that surgery as the key event of his life. "The fall is my favorite season," he wrote in his article. "Perhaps because of the brilliant color of the leaves, and that the chilly wind undresses the dogwoods. Or fall may be my favorite season because three years ago I used to look out my hospital window and long to be outside. This memory reminds me of the healing God worked in my life in November of 1975."

We all love the blooming of new life in the spring and the pleasant, relaxed days of summer. But sometimes God does his greatest work in a life during the fall—in times of disappointment and pain.

4
HIGH-SCHOOL CLASS

*B*Y WHAT DEVICE MAY A FATHER DIVINE THE SPIRITUAL LIFE OF his son? the beasts battled, the cliffs scaled, the heights ascended? Had I Merlin's magic mirror, could I locate Sandy's pilgrimage through some spiritual geography? Sandy did not talk much or easily about himself. We heard more often about his disappointments and defeats in high school than about his victories and achievements. If he got a ninety-four when he thought he might have gotten a ninety-eight or one hundred, we heard about it. If he got one hundred, we heard nothing.

And yet he was a teen-ager—enduring that clumsy, contradictory time between childhood and adulthood. He could be serious and silly, responsible and irresponsible, considerate and vain, all in the course of a single day. But Sandy always had a focus, a direction and seriousness that set him apart.

With a new blue coat and tie, an eleven-year-old Sandy came every night to his Uncle Billy's Charlotte crusade, taking notes carefully. Adults remarked on his precocious attention to everything his uncle said. At twelve, he refused to play a championship little league football game on Sunday. Jeanie and I would have permitted it, but he made the decision on his own.

Nephew of Billy Graham, son of Leighton Ford, Sandy was, in a sense, heir of a tradition. While he was growing up, our home was visited regularly by missionaries, pastors, evangelists and others who had given their lives entirely to Christian ministry. Many of these were around enough to influence Sandy; all of them added to his warehouse of role models.

The single, strongest influence on Sandy outside the family was probably Cliffe Knechtle. He studied at nearby Davidson College and spent almost every weekend with us. Cliffe was a disciplined student, a hard-working basketball player on the Davidson team and a dedicated Christian. Though he came from a well-to-do Connecticut family, possessions meant little to him. Sandy absorbed all this, looking up to Cliffe like an older brother who affected Sandy's attitudes toward girls, clothes, study and the Christian life.

He thus grew up with a deep, inexpressible sense of honor, a code to live and die by, a gospel to tell, an assignment to carry out. There must have been times when this was a burden to him. But during his high-school years, he came to shoulder this mantle deliberately, consciously as his own. These were the years too when he was learning the lessons of grace. In the hospital, he had received the gift of love from many people. He had received life from God. Thereafter, he was in process—and it was a long process, with many setbacks—of learning that life is not ultimately a matter of achievement, but a gracious gift. This realization began to soften his sometimes extreme propriety and excessive expectations of himself and others.

His high-school choir director aptly observed that Sandy "majored in life." In that course Sandy took as his textbook the Bible, convinced that in it he had the key to true life. Jeanie remembers knocking on the door to his room which had been quiet for an evening. There he sat, as he often sat, in his big, gold-painted rocker, with his Bible in his lap.

Sandy was born the year John Kennedy was elected president. By the time Sandy had entered his teens, two Kennedys and Martin Luther King, Jr., had been slain, Neil Armstrong had stepped on the moon, Vietnam had become a household word and Watergate had burst upon the nation. The sixties and seventies have been described as an age "when dreams and heroes died." Yet at a time when most were in post-Watergate cynicism and descending into the narcissism of the seventies, Sandy was pondering, in the fitful and supercharged way of youth, the wisdom of the fear of the Lord. Little wonder then that he seemed so out of step with the times, so separate, apart from his peers, as they all observe. More wonder that he was likewise so popular.

"Hey, Sandy, want to go see a movie?"

It was David Shipley, Sandy's best friend in high school, calling on a weeknight.

"Hey, David! Let's see. I've got twenty minutes more of English, fifteen of history, and twenty-five of biology. . . . Yeah, I can go."

Time was critical to Sandy. It was almost a compulsion with him. But he had to be disciplined with his studies because he was not a natural scholar. Everything came hard to him because he was such a perfectionist. He precisely allocated his time to each subject and project. Kevin could do in half an hour what it would take Sandy hours to do. When Sandy was in high school, we got him a table six or seven feet long so he could spread his work out on it. Kevin never used a desk. When he did do homework, he sprawled out on his bed; it was easier for him.

Sandy's concern to use every moment arose in part too from his itch to do it all. By high school, running was his sport, and this required daily training and many weekend meets. He even worked part-time and summers at *Phidippides,* a running-shoe store named for the messenger who ran twenty-six miles to Athens to announce the victory at Marathon and then died of exhaustion. Sandy was president of his class all three years. The church youth group took a lot of time. And studies did too, especially since he was frustrated by anything less than his very best performance.

"Gaah!" I can still hear him behind the closed door of his room upstairs. He would throw his pencil, slam his books and stamp his feet in exasperation. After reading some of his school papers I suggested that he write more simply, but he insisted that the teachers wanted something else. So he wrote long, tortuous sentences, jammed with words fit to choke a horse. He worked hard to develop a good, clear style. By the time he got to college, he was producing first-rate essays, but it took a lot of hard, disciplined work.

While Sandy's discipline with time allowed him to do much that he could not have done otherwise, it also had an overdemanding edge at times. Once Sally Wade and Sandy were at home while Jeanie and I were away. Kevin, who was about eleven then, was at a friend's house. He called to ask Sally if he could stay a little longer. She told him he could stay another fifteen or twenty minutes. "Well, which is it?" Sandy asked Sally. "Fifteen minutes or twenty minutes?" Sally told Kevin twenty minutes.

When Kevin was more than twenty minutes getting home, Sandy read the riot act to him: "Time is important, Kevin! Time is important!"

Sandy certainly had time for his friends, though. There was Donny Little who met Sandy in church and was his best friend during boyhood days. They loved to ride their bikes and play tennis together. There was big Billy Dew who was always smiling. And, of course, there was David Shipley who had moved with his family from Philadelphia. They first met during David's sophomore year when he flew down to visit his grandmother in Charlotte. Sandy's first impression of David was that he was a little "wild" because his shirt was unbuttoned lower than most. But they soon found they had much in common and became fast friends.

Sandy introduced David to Billy Dew on a trip to the lake with the church youth group. At bedtime, Sandy came up with the idea that it would be hilarious if they sprayed shaving cream all over Billy's sleeping body. In fact, it would be even neater if David would do it!

"No way, Sandy," David protested, "that big palook would smash my face in."

But David quickly changed his mind when Sandy started spraying the shaving cream all over Billy. Quickly David moved in to take his turn just as Billy woke up. He slowly wiped cream off his face and growled, "I am going to kill someone." The next day he threw both Sandy and David into the lake.

Sandy and David used to drive through Charlotte with garbage bags full of water balloons, pull up next to a crowded theater line, pelt these sitting ducks and drive off before anyone could respond. They also used to cruise Charlotte scaring people with the PA system in David's car. One night the four friends, Sandy, Donny, Billy and David, drove to the pastor's house and through the loudspeaker announced that the house was surrounded by the police. The pastor's young son got scared, and the pastor's wife came tearing down the street after them. That was the end of their PA prowls.

But David and Sandy quickly picked up another pastime they enjoyed even more—pool hopping. Late at night, they (along with Czar) would jump in one pool after another to see how many they could swim in without being caught. At one of the country clubs when they heard someone coming, they jumped out of the pool and went racing down the golf course in the middle of the night.

"Once, when we were about sixteen," Donny Little told me, "a bunch of us were down at the beach. Someone suggested we go to see *The Rocky Horror Picture Show,* and we all thought that would be a real kick, except Sandy. He wouldn't go. I said, 'Come on, Sandy, it's just a movie. Big deal!' David Shipley got on him too. David told Sandy he didn't know what he was doing. But he would not be persuaded.

"It made me angry. Why does he have to make such a big deal? We were all miffed at him, but deep down we all respected him too. He stuck to his principles—even at sixteen—and we were drawn to that, even though it made us uneasy. He wanted acceptance, he wanted friends, but he wouldn't compromise for it.

"He was so straight I never felt I could put my feet up and relax with him, tell him everything. He always pushed himself, and I was taking things—everything, studies, the faith—pretty easy. Seeing Sandy always made me feel a little guilty.

"At the same time, the one thing people would notice about Sandy immediately—even in high school—was that he cared about you. He'd remember your name, or some little thing about you, and you knew that you'd registered with him, that he cared.

"You got to understand too that Sandy could've gone a very different route—he was popular, good-looking, a jock, honors student. But he chose to live by Christian standards. I remember he quoted from Robert Frost's poem [about] the road less traveled in a speech one time. And that's what he did—he chose the road less traveled."

David Shipley's view was both similar and different: "Sandy was just an ordinary guy—no miracles, no murders—although he *was* extraordinarily conservative. One time, Sandy and I and Billy Dew went to Pizza Hut, and Billy ordered a beer. (He was older than us; we were maybe juniors or seniors in high school.) Sandy got really uptight about that beer. You could tell he was uncomfortable.

"Finally, he said, 'This really bothers me.'

"And Billy said, 'If you want, I'll send it back.'

"Sandy said, 'Yes, I wish you would.'

"So he did. Which shows you how well we got along. He was just more traditional than the rest of us.

"But another side of Sandy came out one night when a group of us were out cruising around Charlotte. We were stopped at a traffic light and a car full of Blacks drives up alongside. Sandy starts jiving in street talk with them. He knew them from school. The rest of us were in private schools [where there were very few Blacks] and didn't know what was going on. We said, 'Sandy, what are you saying?' And he just laughed and kept on jiving till the light changed.

"That thing was with him all the time. I mean his heart problem. I know it hurt him when no one else was with him. We never talked much about it. He was too competitive—just messing around shooting baskets or flirting with girls was competitive with Sandy. Not unhealthy competitive; we cared about each other. His heart was part of his motivation. He was given a second chance, same as people who've lost arms or legs. It was an obstacle; he had to prove to others, but most important to himself, that he could make it. Once one of the wires they'd stitched his rib cage together with was coming loose and sticking out of his skin. He showed it to me. His heart problem was always there."

While Sandy's drive propelled him to throw his racket down if he wasn't playing tennis well, it also propelled him to excellence. He wanted to succeed in perhaps the most demanding sport of all—distance running. Sandy had begun to run seriously before his surgery in the fall of 1975. The very next spring, he went out for track again. Once Sandy was being timed for the mile run. Because of his recent surgery, he was gasping for air as he finished. But because he was Sandy he would not quit, and he nearly collapsed at the finish line. We found out later that Sandy had had another heart flutter. After we checked with the doctors, they said he should wait until the next fall. So in autumn of 1976 and all the next year, Sandy ran cross-country, emerging as the number one runner for the Myers Park Mustangs. The local papers over these two years singled him out as a prep runner worth watching.

With a mother's intuition and concern, Jeanie had never accepted Sandy's return to running after the operation. Questions about what it would do to his heart nagged her, even though the doctors at Duke had assured us there was no reason Sandy should not run again. I could sense her resistance but, knowing how much Sandy wanted to run and what it was doing for his self-image, and knowing also how much I enjoyed watching him, I tried to minimize her fears.

These tensions erupted late one afternoon in April 1978—at the Queen City Relays. I had to be in Fort Campbell, Kentucky, to preach that Friday night, and missed the event of the year. When Sandy collapsed at the end of the distance medley relay, toward the end of his second year of competitive running, we could not view it as an unprecedented fluke. There had been other heart flutters. Sandy survived this attack, and so did my relationship with Jeanie, though it was fiercely tried by our disagreement. But Jeanie became even more opposed to his running.

In the fall of 1978, however, after experiencing a couple more flutters during cross-country runs, Sandy reluctantly agreed with the doctors who by that time had recommended that he not run competitively at the college level. He decided to sit out track the spring of his senior year, and never ran competitively again. As it turned out, his dramatic finish at the Queen City Relays was his last track victory.

Lisa Funderburk met Sandy in 1976 at the *Phidippides* running-shoe store. Lisa was a cross-country runner too. Her family had just moved to Charlotte, so she had few friends. As it happened, Lisa and Sandy had several classes together that fall also. Boyfriends came and went for Lisa in high school, but she and Sandy remained close throughout. Their friendship survived even an irate boyfriend who once skidded into Lisa's drive just as she and Sandy were leaving for a round of golf! Lisa was a regular churchgoer, but not a committed Christian, and she sometimes thought Sandy a bit fanatical.

"He was so serious!" she said later. "I've never known anyone else so singleminded and focused. I wanted to say, 'Come on, Sandy! Life is not that serious. Lighten up!' Now I understand it was because of his faith.

"I'd never prayed aloud in my life, except bedside prayers and blessings at meals. But even then, praying was as natural for Sandy as drinking water. But he didn't always handle his faith so well. I remember one time in high school when Sandy just shoved a tract at me without even looking at me, and walked away.

"But he could goof off too in class, especially in labs. One day he had his head down and his hair caught fire in the Bunsen burner, and he didn't know it. I had to beat it out. He just joked about it, and we all laughed. He was such a paradox—so serious, so much fun.

"I think his heart made him serious too. It bothered him more than his parents knew. Once after he'd stopped running competitively, I saw him and I could tell he'd been running! We used to run together a lot. I know he had little heart flutters periodically. So I confronted him. 'You've been running, haven't you?'

"He ducked his head the way he did when he was embarrassed

and looked away. Kind of mentally shuffling his feet like a nervous little boy, he said, 'Look, it's nothing. Just don't say anything to my mom and dad!' "

Jean Carmichael, a chemistry teacher at Myers Park High School, was adviser to the class of 1979. She remembers that class as a transitional generation. With their arrival on the scene, the apathy of the early seventies was giving way to more positive attitudes. Twenty-six members of that class ran for places on their sophomore class council. Sandy was elected class president, a post he won his junior and senior years also. They were able to lead if they were allowed to. So Jean encouraged them to make decisions, with her counsel when needed. But she also let them make mistakes. She had confidence in them.

"He was a born leader," she said. "He had the wisdom to know he couldn't do it all, and he asked people to help. He held the other leaders together with something you couldn't quite put your finger on. When he said he would do something, I never worried about it again; it would be done. And he was fair—I'm sure this is one reason the students made him their leader. He went to great lengths to ensure that every group was included or represented in every activity. But he had a great supporting cast too. They made the decisions, not I. They led, instead of being told what to do."

When she had to miss the council meeting at which they were to choose their class project and plan their graduation, she was not disturbed. She was delighted when they decided their class gift would be an arboretum.

An arboretum for Myers Park High had long been Jean Carmichael's dream. It was not a personal vision of Sandy and the others. But they worked hard on it once it had been decided. One long rainy afternoon, Brad Simpson, a fellow class officer, and Sandy did the final measuring of the area. An arboretum was certainly something Sandy could give himself to with enthusiasm. It accorded with his desire to transcend time, to leave a mark on life that would last.

Jean was less happy, however, on graduation night when, as a surprise part of the program, Sandy made a speech about their class adviser and called her to the platform to receive a pewter plate. "They were supposed to be honored," she later fumed to me. "It was their night, not mine."

But Sandy and the other class officers had learned a great deal from their experience and they wanted to show appreciation. Sandy had learned that leadership could be lonely. His already strong sense of responsibility and follow-through had grown. Both before and after large class parties there had been occasions when the only ones who showed up to do the decorating or clean up were Brad, Miss Carmichael and Sandy with his brother Kevin.

No one can lead without overcoming disappointments, and student government provided Sandy with another opportunity to learn this. His senior year he had set as his goal to be president of the student body. But so had another gifted classmate, Jimmy Henderson. Sandy was sure his fellow students would recognize his record of leadership and that he would win. According to the rules in Charlotte's integrated school system, if a student of one racial group won the presidency, then the top vote getter among the students of the other race would become vice president. But the school constitution also stipulated that the president must get at least fifty-one per cent of the vote. No one won a clear victory in the primary and the run-off had to take place between Jimmy, Sandy and one of the Black leaders. As soon as Sandy pulled into the driveway that afternoon I could read the result in his face. He had lost, though no one had gotten fifty-one per cent of the vote. He was more than disappointed; he felt rejected. What he regarded as the unfairness of the election requirements was eating at him.

He must have spent most of an hour walking back and forth in our backyard out by Czar's pen. Sandy was mad at himself and was mad at people. "Dad," he burst out, "I've never succeeded in anything. Nothing I've ever tried has gone right."

I tried to put this into perspective. What about being elected class president? What about the *A*'s he had received? What about his prizes in woodworking? The races he had won? And the trophies upstairs? The friends and family that loved him? But through the lens of his emotions he had lost a major battle in his fight for self-esteem. Though, by his own testimony, he had learned through his operation several years earlier not to base his self-esteem on success, here he was—still struggling with an eight-year-old's self-doubt.

Jean Carmichael was upset too. "I knew he was disappointed. He shared this with me. And I was disappointed for Sandy. I wanted him to be class president. But he took these situations and built on them. He didn't allow them to become stumbling blocks."

We wondered whether Sandy, having lost the race for student body president, would run for class president. We talked about it but he would not tip his hand. As the weeks went by until the next election, we forgot about it.

Then one afternoon Doris Coble, a neighbor down the street, called Jeanie. "What do you think about Sandy's speech?" Jeanie didn't know what she was talking about. Always before when Sandy had a speech to make he would go over it with me, both for content and style. But this time he had made the decision on his own. What resulted, his classmates and teachers still talk about.

Sandy stood on the stage at Myers Park in front of his classmates to make his final election speech. With the easy infectious grace that marked his public speaking, he made a typical self-deprecating remark that got them chuckling. Then he grew serious, "This may be the last chance I will ever have to talk to some of you, my fellow seniors," he said. Gasps. A few had misunderstood. In light of his heart problem, they thought perhaps he was seriously ill. But Sandy had something else in mind.

"I would like to ask for your vote. As you know I have been involved in student government, and I think I have done a good job for you, and I think I can again. But that is not why I am up here today. Because this may be my last formal speech, I want to tell you what is the most important thing in my life." And then, in brief but moving terms, he told about the serious surgery he had in junior high, and how through that his faith had been strengthened and had become the most important thing to him. "Jesus Christ filled a void in my life. If you have a void in your life, why don't you consider him too?"

He sat down. There was a moment of stunned silence. Sandy told us later that when he decided to make that speech, he knew he would risk losing. He thought he probably would. Instead, someone started to applaud and then most of his class rose to give him a standing ovation. Some criticized. Others said it was the best speech they had ever heard. Sandy won the election by a landslide.

To touch the lives of other people in a deep and significant way it takes more than talent, strategy and courage. It takes an indefinable sense of caring. God was putting into Sandy's life a winsomeness that was felt and noticed. Ted Wilson, one of his Myers Park teammates, said that what Sandy was could "come only from the heart. You could feel it from the moment you met him. You can't be liked by everyone. Sandy was the exception. He fit in comfortably without sacrificing any of his beliefs or morals."

Through all these years beat the rhythm of Sandy's running feet. He continued to run, not competitively, but for the love of it. And periodically his heart, faltering and fluttering, reminded him: Live today; the flesh is weak and transient; tomorrow is not guaranteed. So he gave every day, every activity, every person his best effort because every day, *any* day could be his last lap, the final leg of the race.

But now, with high school behind him, the future lay open before him. The first step was college, and he was ready.

5
NEW SCHOOL,
NEW LOVE,
NEW MISSION

W*E UNDERSTAND YOU'RE PRETTY STRAIGHT, SANDY. IS THIS* because you're Billy Graham's nephew, Leighton Ford's son?"

Spring 1979. Sandy was choosing a college. He had considered many, applied to a number, visited several. The University of Virginia wanted him, but it did not seem quite right to Sandy. He was rankled when Duke turned him down. Wheaton College promptly accepted him, and he thought long and prayerfully about this college that both Jeanie and I had attended. His Christian studies and the contacts he would make there would be invaluable if he headed for the ministry. Then, in the midst of these choices, the matter seemed to be resolved—he was nominated for a Morehead Scholarship. The Morehead is a scholarship to the University of North Carolina, Chapel Hill. It would pay all his costs for four years, and provide unusual summer employment opportunities and experiences in the United States and abroad.

Sandy was being grilled by the final, national selection committee in Chapel Hill. He had made it through the local and regional interviews easily, being judged according to four criteria: academics, leadership, sports and character. Sandy had prepared well, having been tutored by a battery of teachers and former Morehead winners.

He was a little uneasy, dressed up in clothes still too new to be comfortable. Just the day before, we had bought a sport coat and wool slacks for him. Sandy always wanted to look good. He was neat and clean, always wore a belt and had his shirttail tucked in. But he was not a clothes horse and stubbornly resisted buying anything new. There were better things to do with one's money. But the Morehead committee required all nominees to dress up the entire weekend during these final interviews. He looked good as he cleared his throat to answer the sticky question about why he was so straight.

"I'd like to think it's because I'm *God's* son."

A Morehead Scholarship would give Sandy opportunities he would not otherwise have. "Moreheads" were distinguished in their fields; the scholarship was a springboard to further opportunities. Sandy wanted this scholarship. He knew he had a good chance; he had been the first choice of the regional committee.

"If I was walking down the road," another committee member was asking, "and got hit by a car and was killed, would I go to hell?"

"I don't make those judgments," Sandy replied. "That's in God's hands."

He had done well; we were proud of him. Returning from Chapel Hill, Sandy was confident, but Morehead or no, he had decided that Carolina was going to be his school.

I was in Australia when the final results were mailed. Sandy was at school. Jeanie opened the envelope. "Dear Sandy, We regret to inform you. . . . " She could not believe it. How was she to tell Sandy? Eager to hear the results, he called from school. "Sandy, you didn't get it." Silence.

When he got home, the hurt was evident. Why had he lost? Was it his beliefs? Was it his inability to compete in college sports? We would never know. But very quickly Sandy accepted it; his attitude amazed Jeanie. It was harder on me than it was on Sandy. I wrote him from Woolongong, Australia: "The honor of winning a scholarship is a poor second compared to the honor of character, of attitude, of how you accept what happens. So while I am as disappointed as you are, your reaction makes me as proud of you and as thankful as I have ever been in my life."

But my letter to Jeanie that day revealed more of my own disappointment than I had let on to Sandy. "I will be honest," I wrote. "Just a few minutes ago I was thinking about it and I cried. Not for Sandy, but for me. I'm proud of his attitude and I believe God has what's right for him, and I sort of hope that might be Wheaton for a couple of years. . . . But I think more of me is wrapped up in Sandy than I have ever allowed myself to feel. That goes for his running too. I guess it's all tied up with the need to achieve, to feel more worthy in achieving than in not achieving. This is the feeling that I still have to deal with, just as much at my time of life as Sandy at his, maybe more.

"Sandy will do great wherever he goes, and God's grace is enough for him. I am still learning that it is enough for me too! I shouldn't need to prove anything, should I? You taught me that. I know you accept and love me, period. That's a lesson in grace. Anyway, I had to share this with you. I'm fine. I'm more proud of Sandy for his attitude and acceptance than I would be if he had won the Morehead."

Fathers and sons. In the same school—the school of grace.

There are no scholarships, and you graduate only when you die.

College begins early in the Carolinas. The third Sunday in August we loaded Sandy's car after church and I drove with him to Chapel Hill. He had missed the full benefits of a Morehead. But because he had made the finals, his tuition and fees, though not his housing and other expenses, would be paid by the Morehead foundation.

The summer had been fun. After a trip to Myrtle Beach with friends, Sandy had joined Jeanie and me at the Lancaster crusade, leading youth meetings and giving his testimony. Later that summer, Kevin, Sandy and I took a "men only" trip to Jim and Anne Price's big old lake home in northern New York. Sizzling barbecued steaks, the crack of rifles as we took aim at tin cans, the pull of muscles as we climbed Mt. Debar to the lookout at the top. A friend of mine calls trips with his children "buying a memory." For me, it was surely that; for Kevin, that climb became a symbol.

As I helped Sandy unpack his things that August afternoon at Granville West, his dormitory, a girl from Black Mountain, North Carolina, was doing the same in neighboring Granville East. Susan Wheelon occasionally saw Billy Graham in her small North Carolina community where he too lived. Just before she left for school, Billy had suggested she look up Sandy and Debbie Ford. Thinking she would have two of Billy Graham's nieces for friends at Chapel Hill, she was a little surprised when her suitemate, Missy Garrett from Charlotte, introduced her to Sandy.

Susan's room seemed like a Christian fortress, bedecked with Bible verses, posters and other Christian fetishes designed to ward off the pagan, godless spirit she and many other Carolinians believed prevailed at Chapel Hill. He could see she needed fellowship and was a little homesick. He stayed and talked.

"Sandy, why didn't you go to Wheaton?" That was where Susan

wanted to go but couldn't because of finances. She felt the Lord was alive and working there in contrast to UNC. Later she saw how great a work God was doing at Chapel Hill. Sandy's response to her question helped her eyes begin to open.

"We couldn't fulfill the purpose that God has for us in college if we were anywhere else. That's why we're here."

That night, after establishing with his roommate and suitemates that the tub was for showers and baths, not for keeping beer on ice, Sandy wrote us one of the rare letters we received from him in college. His roommates were nice guys, but they partied a lot. And he had met this cute girl from Black Mountain, "a terrific personality and a great Christian." Then, more seriously, "I think I will become a much stronger Christian here, because I really have to depend on God. This is something I don't think I would have learned easily at a school where everyone is supposedly a Christian (e.g., Wheaton)." After a warm expression of appreciation and love to Mom and Dad—which was easier to say on paper than in person—he closed with a typical, freshman windup. "I still need to talk to ya'll about my allowance."

When Sandy wrote David Shipley early that fall, true to form, Sandy had already established priorities. "All of it [Carolina] is a lot of fun, but my priorities are: 1—God, 2—Academics, 3—Physical Vigor, 4—Social Things." From his occasional letters and weekend telephone calls it soon became clear that one of those "Social Things" was the cute girl from Black Mountain, with whom Sandy would share his commitment to God and his studies.

The first year away from home can stretch family relationships. One night, after a painful phone call to her parents, Susan went out for a walk and ran smack into Sandy. Concerned about her walking alone at night, he decided he just happened to be going the same direction. Susan related the phone conversation. Sandy listened, then shared how special his family was to him. Sometimes communication broke down, but always there was the ability to pray over problems and to say, "I'm sorry."

Through tears, Susan said, "Sandy, sometimes it is so hard for me to look my mother in the face and say, 'I love you.' "

Only half conscious of how difficult this was for him too, Sandy took her hands and started to pray, "Lord, help Susan to understand the love of her parents, however they express it. Father, understanding your will is a long and difficult process, but you promise us your guidance and your love. Thank you, Father God. We know that we need nothing else." Indeed God answered Sandy's prayer as Susan later saw how much her parents did care for her.

On frequent long walks across the Carolina campus they had searching and thought-provoking discussions. Susan asked many questions and Sandy answered them as carefully as he could. But he never answered a question he was not sure about. He would say, "I don't know," or, "Let me study on it and find out what God is really wanting me to share with you about that."

One afternoon on Franklin Street they met several men collecting money for an unstated "mission." Susan plopped some spare change in the can. As they walked on, Sandy asked, "Susan, why did you do that? Do you know what their mission is?" She didn't. "Do you know why they are collecting money?" No. "Susan, please be careful. Giving is a wonderful thing to do for God. But know what you give to. Know for whom you are giving it. Make sure the ministry you are giving to is of God." Susan laughed but Sandy would not let it drop. "Susan, how do you think the Moonies got started, for heaven's sake?"

The week before the first football game that fall, Sandy came over to Susan's room. "Well, you know, there's a football game next Saturday and I thought you might like to go." He said it casually, with a big grin on his face. Susan was sure he knew what her answer would be. But she stuttered around for a moment before saying, "I'd love to!"

As they began to date, she studied him. She saw a young man who was forever in the spotlight whether with Christians or not. Someone was always calling on him to pray or talk or asking him a leading question. He coped with it well. He would come back with a simple gesture that people knew was from his heart. But just as easily, he made people laugh. One of his friends said, "He was as much of a clown as a Christian."

"He had a God-given talent for making people feel at ease," Susan wrote us, "for making people satisfied with where they were right at that moment, making them want to be nowhere else."

That may have been easy enough with the girl he was dating and with Christian friends, but being an effective witness on a secular campus is not easy. Sandy and Deb drove to Grandfather Mountain, North Carolina, to meet Jeanie, Kevin and me over the Labor Day weekend. He spoke candidly about the heavy drinking and the casual sex that surrounded him.

While we were relaxing that weekend, word came to us that our close friend Arthur DeMoss had died. He was fifty-four. We were all sobered, for our families were close and Art was one of the most dedicated Christians we knew. Jeanie and I flew to Philadelphia for the memorial service where I was to speak.

Later I wrote to Sandy about it. "It was especially moving to see the scores of people who stood up to say they had accepted Christ as a result of Art's personal witness. That is a lot more important than being president of National Liberty Insurance Company. That is why I'm so glad you are staking out your Christian position right away at Carolina, like taking Scott and others to church. It is so vital to let that stand be known—other pressures can so subtly tone down what you believe. I am praying you will have a warm but direct way of sharing Christ. Away from home you will need to keep in contact with the Lord daily to find the inner strength you need."

Several days later I wrote him again with some information for a paper he was doing on the political situation in Quebec. I closed my letter with a quote from Jim Elliot, a missionary killed by the Auca Indians in South America. When Elliot was twenty-one and a student at Wheaton he wrote, "Lord, make me a crisis man, not a milepost in the way but a fork in the road, so when people meet me they will have to decide about Christ in me."

A fork in the road does not shout at travelers, it merely shows them there are two different ways to go. Early that year there was a PJ party at Granville East. PJ was a mixture of punch and liquor, and you were supposed to dress in your PJs and drink PJ. Susan was mortified and determined that she would not go to a party whose sole purpose was to drink as much as possible as fast as possible. Sandy laughed. "Well, you know, we *have* to meet people!" So he put on his bathrobe over his jeans and Susan put on a long flannel nightshirt over her shorts.

"I never really thought a lot about social drinking," said Susan. "How does that fit into our witness?" Sandy said he had not thought much about it either. But because social life was strategically important at Carolina, it was something they were going to have to face. While Susan had a strong faith, she was not used to sharing it with others. So they bought a six-pack of Pepsi and carried it nonchalantly into the party, just as everyone else was carrying their PJ or beer. That six-pack of Pepsi became a trademark for both of them.

Thus, Sandy's legalism began to soften. In early high school, for example, the thought that a homosexual might approach him elicited a hostile, even violent reaction. He had no tolerance or compassion. But during Sandy's freshman year at Chapel Hill, one of his friends, Ellen, had a roommate who was a lesbian. Before coming to Chapel Hill, Ellen hardly knew what a homosexual was. Threatened and perplexed, she was quite unprepared to live with one. Her usual sensitivity was paralyzed. When Barbara, her gay roommate, announced that she was joining a local gay association, Ellen panicked.

"*Now* what do I do?" she asked Sandy. "Good grief, I couldn't talk to her *before!*"

"Have you prayed about it?"

Ellen had not. So they did. They prayed for the ability to see from Barbara's viewpoint.

One night Sandy came over. "I have decided that we don't talk to Barbara enough. Have you ever thought about how lonely she probably is?"

"But, Sandy, I *do* talk to her."

"You should talk to her more. Not just good morning or how are you. You should really talk to her. Get a real feel for how she thinks and feels."

With one eyebrow cocked, "Sandy, you *know* what she thinks and feels?"

"We know only what we *think* she thinks and feels."

That night when Barbara returned, Sandy sat down and talked with her. They found out she was from a religious family; she knew the Lord and his will in her life. She had heard about the Inter-Varsity Christian Fellowship group that Sandy was already a part of, but no one had ever invited her. During the next hour and a half they talked about her life and about Christ in a comfortable way that laid the groundwork for a more open and relaxed relationship among the three of them.

When Sandy went to Chapel Hill, Lisa Funderburk went to Duke, just fifteen miles away in Durham. She often called to cry out her problems to Sandy. He had nothing to say on these occasions—no advice, just a sincere and very serious, "I'll pray for you."

A fat lot of good that'll do, Lisa thought. Can't you think of something more concrete? She was, she says, "just a Methodist" then, and only that year beginning to awaken to a personal faith in God. A year later she would be calling Sandy to *ask* him to pray for her. But during their freshman year she was impatient with his sober piety. Even the following spring when Sandy, in what for him was a major expression of affection, held her hand, she would inwardly roll her eyes and think, "Oh, Sandy, get into the twentieth century!"

Sandy had always been rather too serious—especially where girls and spirituality were concerned. We used to think that he needed to lighten up a bit, but this seriousness was a part of his natural intensity. To Lisa it seemed that sometimes he was not quite present, as if he lived simultaneously in two worlds: present but not unconditionally committed to *this* world. "Sometimes I wanted to shake him," she said, not because he was absent-minded but because he was deeply involved in another level of reality. Even his high-school buddies felt this otherness.

But once that year when Lisa called Sandy in despair, pouring out her freshman complaint to him, he did give her some advice. He began in his quiet serious way to counsel her. One of the outstanding landmarks on the Duke University campus is Duke Chapel, its tall, gray-brown tower visible for miles above the wooded campus. She should go to Duke Chapel, Sandy counseled, and there quietly put herself into a right frame of mind. (Impatient, Lisa anticipated what he would tell her to do there: Pray? Talk to the campus chaplain? Read Scripture? What?) Having thus prepared herself, Sandy continued, she should then climb the tower and jump off. For a moment Sandy's serious tone hung in the air between them. Then it and Lisa's burden were obliterated by the explosion of their laughter.

As the semester wore on and homecoming weekend approached, Sandy was digging hard into his studies. He was particularly intrigued with a seminar on international politics. He made a presentation on Vietnam and Cambodia. He had also been asked to serve as missions chairman for his Inter-Varsity chapter and was looking forward to the Urbana missionary convention at Christmas.

But his happy freshman year suddenly clouded over when a high-school friend of Susan's came up from Clemson for the homecoming game. To Susan he was just a friend she had dated two or three times. But he was handsome, and Sandy was jealous.

Whether because of general insecurity or because two girlfriends in high school had broken up with him, Sandy was ambivalent toward girls. He liked them—especially if they were cute. But he would not go out of his way to accommodate them. How many times Jeanie advised him to call his girlfriends on the phone and talk to them for five minutes or just drop by and say, "Hi," or send them a funny little card. He learned to take her advice, but it wasn't easy. If they wanted to call that was fine, but he was not going to. On the other hand, if at the church youth group he saw his special girl talking too long to another fellow, he would come home dragging, sure that she no longer liked him.

Jealousy struck again when Ted came up from the University of South Carolina. By this time, Susan and Sandy were a regular item, so Susan talked to Sandy about going to the game with Ted instead of him. His eyes shrouded, and he said quickly—a little too quickly—"Sure, fine."

That Friday night, Susan and Ted went out with some of her friends. Sandy was studying. When she returned at 12:30 A.M., her roommate had posted a series of notes: "10:00—Sandy called." "11:15—Sandy called—call him." "11:50—Sandy called." "Call Sandy when you get in." When she phoned, there was an urgent tension in Sandy's voice.

"Susan, I've got to talk to you."

"O.K. Why don't we get together for breakfast in the morning?"

"I need to talk to you tonight, Susan, not tomorrow. I'll meet you outside on the basketball court in ten minutes."

"But, Sandy! It's almost one o'clock!"

"I know what time it is. I've got a clock."

Susan sat on the brick wall surrounding the basketball court watching Sandy pace. "Sandy, I'm tired!"

"No doubt!"

"Why are you angry?"

"I'm *not* angry. I'm totally bemused." The darkness hid the feeling in his eyes, but his voice betrayed it. "Susan, you know the strengths I have aren't of this world, but my weaknesses are. I think right now my weakness is most evident to you, and I don't apologize for that because I have thought a long time about the way I feel." He stopped pacing and looked at her. "Susan, I think—I've thought about it a long time and I think I have really fallen in love with you in a very special way. As much as I can with God as my Father, I love you very much, and I want you to know that. Perhaps this is not a good time to tell you but I just couldn't go to sleep until I did."

Both Susan and Sandy were too innocent to analyze the timing of this confession—just when Ted had come to Chapel Hill. Susan was thinking that nobody had ever given her such a gift. She was speechless. She could neither cry nor laugh. She reached out, hugged Sandy and said, "Oh, Sandy, thank you so much."

The air was cleared. Sandy's birthday came a week later. She made him a chocolate cake which, they agreed, was the worst cake they had ever eaten. Perhaps the pigeons would enjoy it better. They sang together tunes from *The Sound of Music* and were happy. Susan also cross-stitched for him an old well, a landmark at Chapel Hill. Over it she put the proverb, "Above all else guard your heart for it is the wellspring of life." But she did not realize that she was not guarding her own heart so very well. She had become so dependent on Sandy that God and Sandy had grown into one in her eyes. Instead of going straight to God with her problems and praises, she was going straight to Sandy. Neither of them realized that feelings of jealousy might have come because one or the other had forgotten that only God may be number one.

When exam time came tension began to eat away once more. Sandy was positive that his hard work throughout the term was going to pay off. But Susan was unsure of herself, especially in several classes that were fully dependent on final exams. The pressure got to her and to their relationship. One night she said, "Sandy, I am just fit to be tied." He tried to laugh it off, but she was not buying. "Look," she said, "I feel deeply for you. I love you a lot but there has just got to be some way in the situation I am in—with the grades I have right now—something has got to give. I want to love you, Sandy, but I can't right now."

He looked stunned, and said, "If you love somebody, that's selflessness. If you work hard for grades, then you are doing that for Christ. The pressure you feel is yours. If you give it to the Lord he will handle it."

Susan snapped, "It would be very different, Sandy, if I were as intelligent as you are."

"I think you should take a nap or something. I'm going home to read." He left.

That night Sandy sent a note by a friend. "Susan, I read this today and thought about us. This is very important. I want you to read it and I want you to understand it. It is exactly how I feel." From an Inter-Varsity newsletter, he had copied this: "We all long to give ourselves completely to another. A sole relationship with another to love thoroughly and exclusively. But God to a Christian says, 'No, not until you are satisfied, fulfilled and contented with being loved by Me alone. Give yourselves totally and unre-

servedly to Me, having an intensely personal and unique relationship with Me alone. Only by discovering that in Me is your satisfaction to be found, will you be capable of the perfect human
relationship that I have planned for you.' "

Oh, Lord, Susan sighed, *why do you always chastise me through
Sandy?* She had herself expressed this same conviction to Sandy
many times. Now in someone else's words, her own thoughts
boomeranged and nailed her to the wall. She was chastened but
thankful.

That Christmas was dominated by the Inter-Varsity Missionary
Convention at the University of Illinois, Urbana 79. Deb and
Sandy went as student participants; Jeanie and I went as guests
of Inter-Varsity.

With characteristic energy, Sandy set out to learn all he could
at Urbana about his job as missions chairman. He had a special
desire to understand the role of missions in the turbulent modern
world. And he wanted to discover God's plan for his career. With
an intense interest in political science and economics, he
watched closely what was happening in the world. Fifty Americans were being held hostage in the embassy in Teheran. The
Soviet Union had just invaded Afghanistan. Millions had been
exterminated in Cambodia and Laos. A revolution was underway
in Nicaragua. He was considering a career in law or politics, and
had talked of trying to find a government intern job in Washington, D.C., the next summer. But perhaps God had a different plan
in mind. If so, Sandy wanted to know.

After an early morning Bible study with an African and a Canadian student, Sandy walked with fifteen thousand other students
through subfreezing temperatures across the Illinois campus,
head buried in the hood and hands thrust deep in the pockets
of his blue wool jacket, to hear the Bible messages by John Stott
of London. During the afternoons he took the workshops "Choosing a Mission," "Development in Evangelization," and "The Place

of Missions in an Inter-Varsity Chapter."

"What is your biggest dream about the greatest impact your chapter can make in Christ's global cause in the next three years?" he asked himself. His answer: "Option for each member to serve. Small group to adopt a missionary."

The night Billy Graham spoke on "A Magnificent Obsession" some words made a special impression on him. He wrote in his notebook, "The word 'Christian' appears three times in the New Testament. (Each time it deals with suffering—Acts 11, Acts 26, 1 Peter.) It may mean dropping a girlfriend. It may mean dying."

Special seats near the front were reserved for the guests. Usually before a plenary session in the huge hall, Sandy would check in, let us know how things were going and chat with us for a few moments. Several times we invited him to sit with us in that special section since there were extra seats, but he always would thank us and say, "No, I think I'll go sit with my friends. They're expecting me."

During the free times, he made new friends, talked with missionaries and, in a crowded TV lounge, joined other UNC students to watch their team beat Michigan in the Gator Bowl. They cheered so loudly and so late that some of the more sober staff were upset that these raucous Carolinians had disturbed a prayer meeting in a room next to the lounge.

Before leaving, students were asked to fill out an evaluation telling the most significant work God had done in their lives at Urbana 79. Sandy wrote, "He has shown me the need to spend more time with him everyday than I am presently doing. He has also given me more insight in what world evangelization really is. Although I have not made any specific commitment, I am considering going with GEM (Greater Europe Mission) on a Eurocorps summer program. I have made a commitment to bring what I have learned to my chapter as . . . missions chairman."

The Urbana conference was also to have a more personal effect on our family. On the way to the convention his bus from Charlotte had stopped in the middle of the night at a truckstop in Kentucky. A charter bus from Asheville also bound for Urbana pulled in at the same time. Someone pulled at Sandy's sleeve, "Hey, there is a guy on that bus from Asheville that looks just like you. He could be your brother. You ought to meet him."

Sandy walked over and said, "I'm Sandy Ford. Someone said we looked like each other and ought to meet."

"I'm Craig Gourley," came the reply with a smile. They visited a few minutes and Sandy learned that Craig was a Duke graduate presently in medical school at Chapel Hill. Perhaps he sensed that Craig was the kind of guy he would like his sister, Debbie, to meet. In any case, that evening he introduced them, little knowing that he really was playing matchmaker, that his sister had just met her future husband.

Back in Chapel Hill, Susan was eagerly awaiting Sandy's return. "I'm glad Urbana was terrific," she wrote. "I knew it would be. I want to hear all about it! I'll see you Monday—I can't wait!" But she was not ready for what she heard.

"I'm thinking about going to France this summer."

"Sandy, how could you go to France? We'd be apart the whole summer!"

Taken aback by her sharp response, Sandy tried to minimize the damage. "It'll only be for a few months. Think how outstanding it would be to go to France, to sell books, share the gospel, to grow!" He was excited; she was dejected.

Not long into the new semester Sandy was scheduled to attend an Inter-Varsity executive planning retreat. But it conflicted with the date of Susan's birthday. So Susan's plans for a great weekend went out the window. While Sandy's energy was focused on his French prospects, studies and Inter-Varsity work, Susan was also being asked out by other friends. He gave her less attention than before. Were they drifting apart? She wrote a lot in her journal.

Just before Sandy left for the retreat, Susan finally told Sandy, "There is something else I need to talk to you about—I feel that our situation is really not going anywhere and I am not growing anymore and I'm racked with jealousy and I'm easy to anger and I am not really giving you the kind of friendship you need. So I think maybe we should spend less time together."

Sandy looked as if he had been slapped. "What?"

He tried to reassure her and they prayed together and made plans to celebrate her birthday the next Thursday night. They wanted to keep it alive, but things went from bad to worse. Living in Granville Towers, they saw each other all the time, whether they planned to or not. For months they had been in the habit of eating dinner together. Now if they ran into each other and had made no effort to get together, tension would build.

Not all of Sandy's energies and attention were available to devote to this relationship. During an Inter-Varsity executive meeting at about that time, Sandy made this note: "Work as though you will live forever, but work as though you die today."

Clearly he was struggling to find the right tension for Christian living—being faithful one day at a time while having vision for the future. At that same exec meeting, he made a list of "how to live each day," which included meeting regularly with his prayer partner, reviewing his prayer notebook once a week, knowing God and being a channel for God. He underlined the danger of living only in the future, not in the present. Beneath a graph of the years 1980 to 2000, he posed the question, "Am I living as if Christ were returning before 1990 to 2000?" followed by a reference to Jesus' words about taking up the cross *daily*. Inter-Varsity was planning to bring Billy Graham to campus in two years for a week-long mission.

After making some notes on their plans, he wrote, "The system on campus is not . . . Christian, we must restructure the system." That, he noted, would involve a conscious effort to mature in

Christ, growing in prayer, fellowship, effectiveness and witness. It would require the penetration of the dorms and the training of an abundance of leaders for follow-up.

On Valentine's Day, Susan and Sandy's young love finally had to face the painful truth. Susan popped over and gave Sandy a card and a big hug. She promised that things would be better. She said she cared for him and did not want to date anybody else. Sometimes, when she most wanted her freedom, she hoped he would remind her that she really did care for him. Then she told him she loved him.

Sandy looked at her. A pained expression crossed his face. "You know, we might have jumped the gun a little," he said. "No doubt, I love you dearly and I have said it often enough. I really mean it. But it is not the kind of love, I think, that can last through all this turmoil."

Tears welled up in Susan's eyes, but Sandy went on.

"You're right. We definitely need to give each other space. We have to give each other time. We've got to be understanding in that or we will completely lose each other."

Susan agreed. They both knew what was happening.

Their breakup hurt Sandy more than Susan realized. After this talk with Susan, Sandy called home very late. It was very unusual for Sandy to call home except on weekends, and he was upset. As he cried and poured out his anguish to me, I remembered the night in his senior year of high school when he came home late one night, down on himself, and talked to Jeanie. His girlfriend wanted to date other boys, and he could not handle that. He wanted to date other girls, but he did not want his girl dating other boys—he was a chauvinist but had difficulty acknowledging that. So that night, only a little more than a year before this breakup with Susan, Sandy did not feel loved. He felt like a neglected middle child. He got up and walked into my study.

Jeanie followed. "Sandy," she said, "I just want to hug you. I want you to know that we *do* love you."

"Yeah, I guess you do love me—since I'm your first-born son."

"It has nothing to do with when you were born. You're you and we love you, just as we love Deb and Kevin." Jeanie walked over and hugged him. Stiffly, dutifully, he hugged her.

Now he was talking to me about Susan. And though he understood what was happening—that in order for each of them to grow up, they needed to part ways—this breakup dredged up all the insecurities and pain he had hoped were buried.

As spring came on, they saw less and less of each other. When they did come across one another in Granville, there was always someone else with them. They did not talk. A year and a half would pass before they would be ready to build a new friendship.

6
A Carolina Gentleman in Post-Christian France

THE ONE SUN SHINES BEAUTIFULLY BUT WITH A VARIED AND peculiar light in each place on the earth. But a cold rain is the same in Macon, Georgia, or Montmorency, France. It was Sandy's second week in Europe, and it had rained almost every day. It was raining again as Sandy slogged to yet another mailbox to leave one of the thirty thousand tracts the team was distributing. He wondered why he'd come to France—certainly not to splash through rain day after day any more than to get cold, haughty responses to his admittedly butchered French.

On June 28, 1980, Sandy wrote in his journal: "It will be God's mercy that I don't catch a cold by walking around in wet clothes all the time." And a few days later: "I must have reached a thousand mailboxes. My legs are sore. . . . I was feeling half sick, so everything was a hassle."

The first two weeks were hard—physically, emotionally, spiritually. But Sandy had not gone alone to France. He went as part of a short-term summer project known as Eurocorps, one of many Christian missions which give North American students a brief, intense experience of serving and learning about missions abroad. Contacts made with the Greater Europe Mission at the Urbana missionary conference the Christmas before had provided helpful direction. Sandy's friend, Graham Johnston, whose mother had grown up with Jeanie, was also going. That was a bonus. Friends and family pledged financial support, and by early June Sandy flew to Wheaton College for a briefing session and to meet the other members of his team.

Just before leaving for Wheaton, Sandy bought a journal notebook "in hopes," he wrote, making a joke on himself, "that I will have some profound thoughts that will eventually break me even." He had paid $1.65 for it. An analogy growing out of his own keen interest in photography impressed itself on him. "A new Christian is like the development process of a photograph. The negative is the Holy Spirit through which the light (the gospel) shines and imprints an image on paper. The image is there, but you cannot see it until it goes through the chemicals (purifying process in our Christian life) then a clear photograph is seen for the 'finished product.' " He pondered, "What processes in our life would compare?"

The summer in France was to provide a period of intense exposure to a new culture, different and challenging ideas, and demanding work which would be a part of the purifying process in his life.

"Christians need to be careful not to spend *all* their time reading, planning, and fellowshiping," Sandy wrote on June 4. "Christians should take action." The leaders of the Eurocorps team clearly believed that. Almost immediately after the team of eager young missionaries touched down in Amsterdam on June 12, they went into action. A bus took them directly from the airport to the evangelical church in Montmorency (a modest suburb of about twenty-three thousand just north of Paris), stopping only for a brief lunch of mushy peas and tasteless, plastic weiners. Sandy and Graham were quartered in the apartment of a missionary couple, the Stowers, who moved the furniture out of their dining room so the two students could stay there.

"Today we went over our strategy to reach the town of Montmorency," he wrote us rather audaciously two days after arriving. "We are working on a plan to go door to door *(porte en porte)* and distribute literature to about thirty thousand people." Those who showed interest in this initial contact would be followed up by the permanent missionaries led by Earl Sandifer. "We looked at some maps of the region we will be attacking—not unlike a group of guerrilla fighters." And the food was getting better. "The first day or two I wasn't getting much but now I have learned to help myself." With a flourish he signed off in his new language, *"Bonne nuit—gloire à dieu."* He was soon to find that it was easier to write a French phrase in his journal than to witness with it on the street.

During the spring semester of that freshman year, along with his interest in France, Sandy had developed a special interest in Lisa Funderburk. They had been friends for years. But that spring, as she was no longer dating anyone and Sandy's relationship with Susan had collapsed of its own weight, something more than friendship began to show itself. Before returning to Chapel Hill for the second semester, he had dinner with Lisa in Charlotte. During that month he began writing an occasional note to her. He even dropped a hint or two to us about it.

The Funderburks were planning a family trip to England and the Continent that summer, and Sandy was excited about the possibility of having her visit him in France. From the briefing session at Wheaton, he wrote to let her know that their schedule was "fairly flexible" and "they do let us visit with people we know from the States if we let them know ahead of time." He then reminded her that it would take at least ten days for a letter to get to France.

But his mind was also set on the task ahead. "Lisa, there are over thirty-six thousand towns in France without a church." He meant, of course, an evangelical Protestant witness. "I hope our group can change at least one or two of them. Please keep me in your prayers."

As Lisa was still finding her spiritual feet, Sandy ended his letter with a word of encouragement. "I expect this letter will get to you the 14th. The devotions I do then will be centered around this verse and I have the same prayer for you: 'I have prayed for you that your faith may not fail' (Lk 22:32). C. H. Spurgeon says, 'Oh, then Christian, watch well thy faith. If thou canst believe, all things are possible to him that believeth.' "

There was plenty of glory for God that summer, but there was little glory slogging street by street, door to door, canvassing. "I am going through growing pains and I get sick of French," he wrote just two days later. The team members were learning how to present their testimonies in French. Constantly expressing himself in another language was as hard as any job Sandy had ever undertaken. Several of the team members had been in France before and knew the language better. Sandy found himself discouraged and impatient. Becky Samuels, from Fort Worth, teamed up a lot with Sandy because she knew more French. But she remembered that he would be much bolder in attempting to speak the language than she and some of the others, "blurting out" the few phrases he could. At the same time, the French families they witnessed to all seemed to want Sandy over because

"Sawn-dee" seemed to have a knack for making them feel comfortable.

Whether fluent or not, the young Americans soon got their first taste of street evangelism in Montmorency. Three days after their arrival the team went out into the town square where they sang and shared the gospel. Sandy went up to a French gentleman and started talking to him in French. After a few sentences, he asked if he understood what he had said. The man replied, "Non." Sandy said, "Oh," and walked away. Another young Frenchman, Michel, was more understanding and Sandy enjoyed talking to him. But he wrote to Lisa, "I feel that I am taking a continuous French course." He wondered why he was there evangelizing when he could not speak the language. By the next day, he had brightened up and wrote in his journal that he was beginning to understand much of what was said.

The team settled into a routine of hard work which would carry them over the next six weeks. Most days found them distributing literature, taking a simple survey of the religious beliefs of the residents they met in apartments and homes, and giving a basic testimony. They talked to young people in the streets and invited them to a Christian coffee bar or a special film or lecture. Sundays they worshiped in the small evangelical church and from time to time one of the team would speak there.

Like most of the team, Sandy was discovering that the French people by and large were not clamoring to hear the gospel. When he knocked at a door, the person who appeared, if not Catholic, was likely to be an agnostic, an existentialist or a Muslim. There were old folks who seemed to want nothing to do with God or with the young Americans who wanted to tell them about salvation. Two elderly ladies who had been drinking burst into tears every time Sandy asked a question. Some people were interested, but most were merely polite. Some were rude.

One day Sandy and another team member spent an hour and

a half with a woman who was an existentialist. Sandy found it challenging to listen to her ideas and to try to present the gospel to her. After a showing of *Time To Run,* they gave a ride home to two drug pushers from the local high school.

Sandy reflected, "One thing different about the French is that they think a long time before accepting Jesus, whereas for many Americans it comes suddenly." His own beliefs were being tested. "I am still in the process of questioning my faith and its logic. I need to read a lot more."

After two weeks of hard work and little headway, the team leaders, feeling the need for spiritual renewal, called for a day of prayer and fasting. After church they all gathered and prayed for four and a half hours, mostly in French. Sandy found the long meeting tedious and honestly confessed it. "I know I should have a better attitude about it, but I just can't sit that long. My mind begins to wander. If I love God more than others, then I should love talking with him for a long time like I would with my friends—but it is hard sometimes."

The prayer and the hard work were, however, beginning to yield fruitful contacts. There was Chantelle who claimed to be an atheist but had been coming by the church a lot. Sandy felt she was "about to commit her life to the Lord—she was quite charming too." There was a Jewish girl who attended the coffee bar and, with other members of the team, Sandy was able to raise some questions about her belief in God. "It was very encouraging for me to talk in French with her and to start talking to someone with more than a greeting."

The coffee bars were going over well with the young people. The team would sing medleys of negro spirituals and talk about their Christian experiences. One man, who was trying to learn English, said he would return. The next night Fabrice did come back and he and Sandy talked a long time about the gospel. Like many young Frenchmen, Fabrice had a Catholic background.

Though his religious experience did not last long, his interest now seemed to be genuine. He told Sandy, "Just think, if we hadn't met on the street, you wouldn't be leading me toward God." Amazed that it was his American accent and his inability to speak French that initially attracted the young man, Sandy wrote, "God has certainly used my weaknesses."

On their weekly day off, Sandy, Graham and other friends usually would sleep late, get some exercise and then go into Paris. Both the French culture and the French prices impressed them! At the Louvre, he saw the "Venus de Milo" and the "Mona Lisa." In his journal, Sandy noted that he needed to learn more about art, and that Paris was expensive.

The other Lisa was soon to show up and make Paris even more interesting. Halfway through his tour of duty, the Funderburks arrived in Paris. Lisa had forgotten Sandy's phone number and to the exasperation of her parents had to call us from London to get it. But for Sandy and Lisa the day together was worth it.

The day before she arrived, Sandy found it a real struggle to be in the right frame of mind for canvassing. The next morning he went into Paris early to meet the family. The two young people dutifully accompanied Lisa's parents and her brother. As time went on Sandy became doubly frustrated—he wanted to be alone with Lisa, and he desperately needed to find a men's room but couldn't. Block after block, his friends ambled blithely along taking in the sights, while Sandy, too embarrassed to say anything and almost doubled over in agony, could hardly walk. Finally, relief came. He found a men's room. And Lisa's mother, sensing their desire to be alone, brightly suggested that they might want to go on their own and meet the family later.

Hungry after hours of wandering the streets of Paris, they entered a little restaurant. "Sandy had something of the romantic in him," Lisa remembers. "It was in Paris that he kissed me for the first time." Lisa invited Sandy to go back with her to England for

— 79 —

their family trip, but he felt that he could spend neither the money nor the time. He must hold to the priority of his mission.

Sandy did have a growing feeling for Lisa. After she left he wrote, "I really feel we have a fondness for one another (let me be cautious with my words, there have been times in the past when I have used them too liberally)." But he was determined that their relationship "must continue to be founded on the Lord." When he wrote her a couple of weeks later, he reminded her of the phrase in Hebrews: "Let us press on to maturity," and expressed his desire that both their Christian faith and their friendship would continue to grow in that way. He also wrote to her about a phrase from Nehemiah. The people were able to rebuild the wall of Jerusalem because they "had a mind to work." He wanted the Lord to give him the same kind of mind to work in the last days of the campaign, especially as at times they became tired of the repetition and the rejection.

With all his energy he plunged into the closing days of the campaign, trying to make the most of each contact. To his supporters he wrote that "each of the houses in this area has a steel fence surrounding it. Without wanting to stereotype, I see that this image best typifies the French personality: closed and set in its ways. Yet, once inside the 'gate' the French can be very caring." He asked them to pray that the Holy Spirit would open the gates for them to share the gospel. He was encouraged to see it happening.

On the street they met Gerard who was interested in what motivated this team of Americans and was obviously searching for some answers. "It is tiring work but at least you feel you are accomplishing something," Sandy noted with satisfaction. By now he had a better grasp of French and was able to give his testimony at the coffee bar.

Along with the hard work, there were times for relaxation, even for the occasional pillow fight. Although at the beginning of summer he felt he never got enough to eat, he was pleased to write home that on a diet of French bread and pastries he now weighed a hundred fifty-two pounds—the most ever.

By the third week in July, the weather had improved. They had four days of pure sunshine with temperatures in the eighties. He and Graham took off their shirts, put on shorts and, to the astonishment of French neighbors, sat in the backyard of the church playing Uno and trying to get a little bit of a tan.

Perhaps it was on one of those days that he wrote "The Caretaker's Window."

Across the path near where I lounge stands a window,
surrounded on three sides by white plaster,
and the fourth by roof thatched low

Through the window I can see reflections partially,
the red pansies brilliant, the grass blades trimming path
    and wall
as though it mirrors glimpses of reality

One day the caretaker Lord who moves swiftly without haste,
drawn by the call of the trumpet, will throw open the window
so then I will see total reality face to face.

On July 28 the Montmorency project ended. After the final banquet for the team, Sandy wrote, "For the first time I realized how close I had grown to these people." The summer had brought its share of irritations with the conflicts of different personalities and the stresses of the work. But their experiences had bonded them together. Now they had to say good-by. They had ten days free to do what they wanted before coming together again in Paris for a brief tour into Germany. There they would have a final debriefing before going home.

The farewell banquet went late, as such things usually do, leaving Sandy and Graham only a couple of hours sleep before setting off early next morning for a romp through Switzerland and the French Riviera. First stop was a couple of days with the Jean Andrés in Lausanne. They found the city and their hosts utterly charming, and enjoyed visiting the old market, swimming in the lake, picking cherries and getting lots of sleep. The Andrés arranged a ride for them to Geneva. From there they hitchhiked to a Christian camp in the French Alps. This became an unforgettable one-day adventure, involving numerous rides, exasperating waits in the hot sun, and an encounter with a metal worker in Chombrey who bought them a delicious lunch. They finally arrived at Camp of Peaks just before dark.

Having had their fill of hitchhiking, they went with others from the camp by train to Manton, just east of Nice. Their agenda for the next several days was simple: sun, sun and more sun. They wrote letters (Sandy asked his mom if on his one day home before going back to Chapel Hill he could have French toast, pancakes and eggs for breakfast, tomatoes, cucumbers and corn on the cob for lunch and a pizza for dinner), took a train into Italy for pizza and wine, stayed up late discussing the gift of tongues—Graham sure it was not valid today, Sandy not sure—and did some reading. Sandy finished my book *Good News Is for Sharing* and began Paul Little's *Know Why You Believe.* "I need to search out answers to some of my intellectual questions."

On the train back to Paris, Sandy had time to reflect and sum up what he had learned, weaving together summer experiences with issues that had long been part of his life. "One of the things stressed on and on this summer is that . . . God is not primarily interested in saving others but he is interested in a relationship with us. Out of that people will come into the Christian family." Sandy's own faith had been stretched.

One of the older teammates, Florence Fiendach, had talked to

Sandy that summer about his relationship with the Lord. "I asked him if his faith in Christ was truly his own. He told me about the heart problem. . . . I felt that someone much older was talking to me." Daily confrontations with existentialists, Muslims and other unbelievers had challenged him as nothing else ever had. If his faith was going to be real, it would have to be based on something more than family upbringing, culture and personal opinion.

He was also learning the importance of a realistic assessment of his own gifts, of God's direction for his life. He felt he had a gift in public speaking which he should develop. The day before he left for home he wrote, "As I think more and more about my future I am beginning to feel a leading into some type of church leadership." Many of the Eurocorps team felt called to return to France as missionaries. Easy as it would have been to go along with the group's sentiments here, Sandy did not feel this call. "It will have to be a matter of prayer."

"It gave me an opportunity to share the gospel and to . . . ask myself many of the questions that the French people asked me," Sandy wrote early in 1981 to a young woman considering the Eurocorps project. "It gave me a chance to slow down into a different lifestyle and *examine* who I *really* am."

That summer Sandy also learned that faith must be nurtured and acted out in community. True religion was not a solitary thing. Seven pages of his journal are filled with thumbnail sketches of his teammates, noting in each case what he felt were strengths and weaknesses. I wonder at his motivation for doing this. Was it simply the instinct of a leader to evaluate those he had to work with? In each case his inclination to see the good in others is evident; he always ended on a positive note.

Of all Sandy's friendships, perhaps none became closer than that with Graham Johnston. In July 1983, three years later, Jeanie and I were in Lausanne on vacation. Graham was also in Europe that summer, so he joined us in Lausanne and we talked about

Sandy and his summer in France.

I asked Graham why Sandy was so hard on himself at times. Graham thought that it was his perfectionist tendency, in which everything had to go like clockwork and that perhaps Sandy was imbalanced about achieving.

"I'm an achiever too, and I would strive hard, but if second place was all I could achieve then I'd accept it. But Sandy wanted it all so badly. He had such a disciplined lifestyle that he would and could achieve almost all of his goals. But no matter how hard you try, sometimes you won't achieve, and that was very hard for Sandy."

He looked at me. "A lot of the reason was that Sandy looked up to you. You achieved. He wanted to equal or surpass you. It was difficult to be your son. People put him in a box. And Sandy not only took on the expectations of others, but increased them because he was your son. He told me this.

"Dr. Ford, he admired and respected you above all men. There is an unconditional acceptance which a father gives to a son. It doesn't depend at all on achieving or not achieving, but just on acceptance as he is. But at another level, a father says, 'I'm really proud of what you have achieved.' And a son recognizes that that is not something *un*conditional, but something he wants to earn.

"Sandy and I talked a lot about dreaming big dreams for God," Graham told me that day. "We talked about being humble and usable instruments. We realized we had advantageous family situations. But we knew that it still would come down to what we personally did with it."

Listening helped me better understand the "glimpses of reality" which the Holy Spirit had imprinted on Sandy's life that summer—the heightened reality of relationship with God, the deepening self-understanding, the desire for a firm foundation of faith, the importance of close and stimulating friendships. It also reminded me that a glimpse of reality means not only a clear understanding of what is, but larger vision of what God wants to bring about.

Graham gave me a new perspective on something Sandy had written the week before he left France. "It is said that boys have dreams but as they begin to face reality, they no longer have these dreams and just settle down to a normal routine, or that they become disillusioned and simply no longer dream.

"I feel that in this way, I am different from many. I still have dreams of what I would like to do and what life should be. But I am beginning to realize that life to me is really short. . . . Anyhow, I am wondering if I have too many dreams. Maybe I need to narrow them—but I hate to."

Summer 1967: A family picnic (left to right—Kevin, Jeanie, Leighton, Sandy, Deb).

Sandy in grade school.

Above: Sandy (far right) with the Dooners during his trip to Ireland in 1975.
Below: Grandmother Graham (center) with (left to right) Kevin, Jeanie, Deb and Sandy.

The Ford children with their uncle, Billy Graham.

The Queen City Relays at Myers Park High School Track, April 1978. Sandy throws himself across the finish line (above). He collapses after winning the distance medley relay for his team (below).

July 1980: Sandy (front) relaxes with friends on a day off during his summer evangelistic project with Greater Europe Mission's Eurocorps.

Above: Graham Johnston (left) and Sandy deliver one of the thirty thousand tracts the Eurocorps team distributed in the summer of 1980.
Below: Sandy sees the sights of Paris with Lisa Funderburk and her brother Tripp (far left) and father (far right).

Above: Sandy relaxing in France (summer 1980).
Below: September 1981: (left to right) Sandy, Leighton, Kevin and Charles Powe.

Above: Sandy and Lisa Funderburk.
Below: Sandy and Debbie Bowers enjoy Frisbee at Windy Gap.

Above: Kevin, Sandy and brother-in-law Craig Gourley.
Below: Kevin and Sandy at their sister's wedding (May 1981).

Above: Sandy at a UNC football game (October 1981).
Below: A photograph taken by Sandy of Myers Park track.

7
THE SALT
OF GRANVILLE
WEST

*I*T IS A LONG WAY FROM AMSTERDAM TO CHARLOTTE BY WAY OF Chicago. The summer in France had been intense and Sandy had pushed hard. So when he walked down the airport corridor late that August night, he was exhausted. He needed a solid week or two of rest. Instead, he had to leave the next afternoon for Chapel Hill to register for fall classes, and to plunge into Inter-Varsity responsibilities and other projects. Still, he'd never looked so good: tanned from the Riviera, he'd put on weight and wore a jaunty tweed cap.

I had been invited to speak to the opening Inter-Varsity meeting the first day of classes. Jeanie, Kevin and I drove up and were impressed by our first solid exposure to these vital young Christians. Over five hundred jammed a student union auditorium.

Sandy had told us of the vision they had to make the Christian community a visible and viable alternative to typical campus lifestyles. Their eager singing, their close attention as I spoke, their camaraderie—all indicated that God was doing something special on this campus. One of our friends, David Spence, was there that night. He had been a student at UNC in the late sixties, when they felt fortunate to get a handful of people together for a Christian fellowship meeting.

Lisa too had come over from Duke. Sandy neglected her. When Jeanie spoke to him about it later, he defended his inattention, saying that there were so many people he had not seen all summer, he ought to mingle with them and greet them. Yet he also seemed disappointed that he and Lisa had not picked up their relationship as rapidly as he had expected after the summer.

Concerned that Sandy was still very tired and carrying a heavy academic load along with his extracurricular activities, Jeanie wrote him in early September. "We have prayed much for you during these first days of school. We are so thankful for you and for all the assets God has given to you. Dad is so proud watching you grow up. . . . I can see so much of Dad in you. You are so much like he was when we first fell in love 'cept you are more outgoing and better looking!! Hope all is going well. . . . Keep your life balance . . . spiritual, social, academic, physical . . . all so important."

Sandy was now thinking about majoring in international relations. That field could open up opportunities to work in government or multinational corporations, but could also lead into a worldwide ministry of some sort with an organization such as World Vision. We were concerned, though, that Sandy was tired and that his course work was a burden to him. I suggested that he drop a course.

He also began corresponding with some of the friends he had made in France. Fabrice, the young atheist, sent him two notes and Sandy wrote back. *"La joie que tu a vu en nous, c'est une joie qui est venue du Christ vivant. Jesus te donnera cette joie et un direction pour ta vie si tu décide de le suivre."* (The joy which you have seen in us is the joy which has come from the living Christ. Jesus will give this joy to you and a direction for your life if you decide to follow him.)

But joy in following Jesus was becoming harder for Sandy. Just before leaving for meetings in Japan, we visited Chapel Hill for a football game and a church service. Sandy was dragging; his fatigue was obvious. Still he continued to make an impression on many people.

Early in her freshman year at UNC, Jodi Smith had already found college to be something other than she had expected. Her home in West Virginia seemed long ago and far away. She felt like a tropical plant in an alpine world—unaccustomed to the cold harsh atmosphere. Wondering what was missing, she accepted an invitation to a Christian fellowship meeting.

Sunk comfortably and inconspicuously down at one end of an old flowered couch, she looked out at the crowded lounge of the Chapel of the Cross. It was a large "sitting room," meant for church teas, with a mellow, dignified feel to it. The room was abuzz with students who, she suddenly realized, were actually listening to each other.

A thin boy with curly hair separated himself from the crowd and was walking to the unoccupied center of the room. An athlete, Jodi's image of an English soccer player. Expression friendly, mischievous, open, excited, secure. Warm, intelligent blue eyes. She was staring. He was talking.

"Could I have your attention for a minute? My name's Sandy Ford, and, um, I just want to, to thank ya'll for coming out tonight. We're glad you're here, to, uh, take a little study break. I know, I know, we've only been here three weeks but some of us got together and decided to go ahead and start studying anyway!"

A chuckle rippled across the room. Sandy grinned, ducked his head shyly and looked out from under his eyebrows. His classic Carolina attire—cotton button-down, off-white cords, running shoes—matched his boyish openness and pleasant manner. He spoke softly, yet commanded attention, his eyes making contact with others. Every other sentence got a laugh. Yet he spoke with care and conviction, as if he knew a great secret he couldn't help sharing with others.

The rest of the year, Jodi hung around the Inter-Varsity group, learning from the other Christians, watching their lives. In the warmth and humor of their presence she found something she thought she had had to forfeit to what the world called reality. And she watched Sandy that year, for in him she thought she saw a model of a feasible, interesting and directed Christian life that was very much involved in the world.

When Billy Rice left his room and started down the fourth-floor hall of Granville West, he walked past the open door of Sandy's room and saw him standing by his phone. As he approached, it was obvious that Sandy was totally frustrated about something. Billy was a freshman, and had been getting to know Sandy just that fall. He looked up to Sandy as a more mature Christian and respected him for his easy, forthright Christian presence in Granville West. Sandy was fuming, almost violent, but reluctant to explain. Billy's sincere concern released Sandy's pressure valve. He raged about people who promised to help but did not follow through.

A major responsibility had fallen to Sandy in the midst of a heavy semester: he was president of the Phi Eta Sigma honor society, which was responsible for publishing a detailed course description of all the university offerings for the next semester. Sandy was determined to make it more comprehensive than any published to date. But the detail and workload was greater than anticipated and, as so often happens, the actual work fell to a few. Sandy had just been on the phone trying to get Phi Eta Sigma members to help—without success. He was burned. Billy tried to encourage Sandy, glad to be able to give something to this "big brother" who had encouraged him so much in his freshman year.

Sandy was pretty close to caving in. But with help, he got through, and on Friday, October 17, in the evening he wrote the only entry recorded in his journal that entire fall of 1980:

Right now as I sit in the 4th floor lounge I think it is good to write about what has been happening this week because I am learning so many things about myself as I did in France. So bear with me, Sandy, as I try to write through my coughing and wheezing, and also the nearby party at a frat house which never ended last night or it started very early this morning.

This week has been the toughest I remember in a long time. I have had numerous quizzes, a lab exam & a Zoo exam which I did poorly on. I have had Inter-Varsity duties to do and had to finish the PES Course Description. Earlier in this week I felt in a stage which I will call "dream-reality." You know how you feel after waking up in the middle of the night from a dream and are convinced that is what you are doing, or where you are—sometimes it is hard to pull yourself together.

Anyway, last night we worked on the Course Description, and as [I was] afraid, the officers got stuck with the job. It was a flop! I came back in a state of complete discouragement— but thanks to Billy and Lisa who directed me again to peace with the Lord, I know that he will show me the way through today.

And so he did! Somehow the final proofs came together. The course descriptions were outstanding. The next week—midsemester break—Sandy was able to come home and rest. For the first time that fall he was beginning to enjoy life. He thought there was a good possibility that he might be elected program chairman of Inter-Varsity. He was looking ahead to attending the National Prayer Breakfast in Washington, D.C., where he would represent the Inter-Varsity chapter. He was beginning to take more of an interest in his class work, particularly the course in classics in which he was enjoying writing and exploring motifs when he had the time.

In his notebook he compared the patience, humility and composure of Odysseus to Jesus. Although Odysseus was lord of his estate, no one recognized him except his son—a parallel to Jesus, the unrecognized Lord of the earth. When he was taking notes on the *Aeneid,* Sandy was struck by Jupiter's "squandering of his ease" and his rebuke by the gods. Sandy applied that personally, "I wonder if I often take the easy way out and don't pursue things that I am capable of or things that God wants me to do. In fact, I can think of times when I can start dating someone and have to cut back on other things. If I do that now, I could be hurting my future because I am still young and am forming foundations for my life following school. On the other hand, one can't always be preparing for the future because he may not live that long. But I believe there is a timing. A time to prepare and a time to marry."

When I wrote Sandy for his twentieth birthday, the big news was that he was going to have a new brother-in-law. A few days before, Craig had driven down from Chapel Hill to ask me if he and Deb could marry. I wrote to Sandy, "Did you know he was praying that God would lead him to his wife at Urbana last Christmas?" And now that seeming "chance" contact at a roadside restaurant in Kentucky was going to bring into our family another tall, curly haired, young man who looked enough like Sandy and Kevin to be their brother.

Christmas 1980 was the first extended break Sandy had since the previous Christmas. And even then he had spent much of his time traveling to and from the exhilarating but exhausting meetings at Urbana. The accumulated stress showed. He was more than usually quiet, and seemed generally run-down and fatigued. Apart from some good paddle tennis matches with Kevin and an overnight skiing trip, he spent much time alone in his room, sitting in his golden rocker, Bible in his lap. We all enjoyed having Craig with us. But Jeanie and I were concerned that Sandy was withdrawn. I had one long talk with him trying to get him to enter more into family activities. Looking back I can see that for nearly a year and a half Sandy had poured himself into his studies, his friends, his leadership positions and his summer trip to France. He had given all he had and he needed time for his physical, emotional and spiritual reservoirs to be filled again.

The intellectual challenges he was meeting at the university and had encountered in France were still working on him. He and I had one very long talk regarding humanism versus Christianity. The pervasive secular atmosphere of the university, often based on an evolutionary materialism, was getting to him. But it was the whole atmosphere, not any particular question, that bothered him. He was finding that one of the biggest challenges to practicing Christians in the twentieth century is simply a whole way of life that does not reckon with God. Being a Christian in a large state university is very much like being a member of the surfing club at the University of Denver.

By the time vacation was over, he was refreshed and eager to get back to Chapel Hill. Once there he wrote to tell us that things had started out well. It was good to get back with friends. "There is such a need to know the Lord better and I have a burden to share with them." After telling us that he had decided not to major in international studies but rather to go the econ-political science route, he closed, "I just want you to know that I love you and really had a good and relaxing time at home."

His change of mood came in part from the encouragement of his many friends. In one, Martha Vetter, who was several years older than Sandy, he was especially blessed. Martha was a deep woman with godly wisdom. She felt a special responsibility for Sandy. One night when they and several others were at Darryl's—a nearby restaurant—Sandy talked about the sophomore blues and how he was not far enough along to be looking forward to his career. The Billy Graham mission was still a year and a half away. Martha was struck by Sandy's admission that he was weak. He was a young man admired for his leadership and scholarship, but when he was hurting he would say so. They talked about what it meant to be content in the Lord.

That night Martha felt deeply that she needed to pray for him. Lying in bed at the Tri-Delt house, she wrote Sandy a note telling him she would pray for several things: First, that he would be able to think intelligently and speak clearly and well. Second, that he would know God's contentment, particularly when the thrill of school seemed to have gone for a time and he had no special relationship with a girl. Third, for him to rest in the Lord and know the Lord as his strength. As a perfectionist herself, Martha could relate to Sandy since she knew what it was to be hard driving and to have struggles with self-esteem. For the rest of that year, Martha kept her commitment to pray for Sandy. Not for many months would she see how completely God had answered her prayers. But in Sandy's mind the encouragement of his new confidante and prayer buddy was immediate. After the dinner at Darryl's, he wrote in his journal,

Recently I . . . have been going through a time of . . . "depression" or "burnout." It has really been hard at times. I feel like there has to be something exciting happening all the time—and things are not really exciting. I feel that I should be dating someone so that things should be really exciting. But two things are helping me to see what is really going on: (1) Martha Vetter gave me words of encouragement that things are happening this way so that I would find my joy in the Lord and in him alone. She challenged me to take advantage of this time. (2) I have been reading about the period of exhaustion in Kings which Elijah went through and how God helped him.

In the midst of these struggles, Sandy continued to be the salt of Granville West. One fellow, not a part of the so-called Christian group, called Sandy a bridge between two very distinct groups on the hall that year. His relationship with Chip Star was typical. Chip lived down the hall, and he and Sandy had a class on Tuesday and Thursday mornings. One Wednesday night Chip was at a big fraternity party. Chip, who had been known to drink a beer or two every now and then, got in about two or three in the morning. Not surprisingly, Chip did not feel like getting out of bed, so he slept in. After Chip had showered and was finally on his way to class, Sandy was getting back from class. As Sandy was getting off the elevator and Chip was getting on, Sandy said, "Good party last night, huh, Chip?" They laughed and Sandy walked on.

It was a casual kind of remark but it stuck in Chip's mind because for him it characterized Sandy. "It points out something about Sandy that I always liked. He never came down on me or on anybody else for the way they lived their lives. He tried to put forth his beliefs by the way he lived; and if people had questions and they came to him, he was more than happy to answer them. But he was never one to try to force his beliefs on anyone else. With me, if someone is pushy, I tend to turn away from them. But I learned more from him because he was himself and lived his life and respected others."

Jeff Carter, a freshman that year, also lived on fourth floor Granville West. "When Sandy and I first met, my roommate was Billy Rice. After living with Billy for a week or so, I began to notice his unusually strong interest in religion. I decided to ask him why he read his Bible so much. Billy took me to an Inter-Varsity small group. Johnny Chandler and Sandy were the only other familiar faces. I don't remember what was discussed, but I do remember how Sandy impressed me with his knowledge of the Bible and with his ability to relate Scripture to our discussion. I had never seen the Bible used in a way that applied it to our lives today.

"Over the next few days, I grappled with what it meant to be a Christian and I drilled Billy with question after question about his faith. One night, Billy said, 'Why don't you go down and ask Sandy the same questions you've been asking me?' My stomach knotted—I realized how much I looked up to Sandy.

"When he opened the door, I could tell he'd been studying. I felt awkward. I don't remember what I said. Here I had barged in on him, interrupted his homework, and he dropped everything to listen to me. He made me feel competent by the way he answered my questions. My questions were embarrassingly basic—he could have made me feel really ignorant. Before I left Sandy gave me several Bible verses to read that helped in my search for Christ."

When Jeff returned to his room, Billy prayed with him and he became a Christian. As Jeff became involved with Inter-Varsity, Sandy asked him to do little details which were part of Sandy's responsibilities as program chairman. "He began to call me Toby, and I called him Massa because of my being his 'go-fer' boy."

Those Christians who looked at Sandy, who admired his calmness and confidence, wishing they had it all together so they could have a stronger influence, might have been surprised—and perhaps helped—to look over his shoulder on May 1 and see what he was writing in his journal. "I have a lot of feelings cooped up inside, and I long for someone to really share with. What I mean, is that I am still very confused about my faith in Jesus and the way the professors here, in general, only allude to Christianity as a passing trend in society. For many months now I have been concerned about this very issue and it seems to keep building up inside me. I cannot understand why I do so much with Inter-Varsity and talk freely about the Lord with others when I have my own conflict going on inside.

"How can I expect not to question the faith when I only have a Sunday-school understanding of it, and have a secular college education behind me? Perhaps I am making a 'simple faith' too hard, yet, it it's really true, how come I can't approach it intellectually? God promises that if we seek him he will reveal himself to us. I sure hope it happens quickly."

He hoped that attending the C. S. Lewis Institute in Washington, D.C., in a few weeks would help him to resolve some of these issues. Another help was the role models he found at a quarterly fellowship meeting he was invited to join. Most were men in their thirties who were successful in their fields and zealous for God. He found it refreshing to talk with them about the philosophies he was encountering on campus.

One of the men, David Spence, encouraged him to look into the qualifications for a Rhodes Scholarship. Others had suggested it to him before. He found the thought tempting. It kept recurring to him even as he wrote his final exams and prepared to leave for home. The last note he wrote to himself before leaving Chapel Hill showed that thoughts of this prestigious scholarship had not kept his mind from more weighty matters: "By the way, I saw Debbie Bowers in the library tonight. She is a beautiful girl!"

8
THE DYING DAYS OF SUMMER

*S*ANDY RAN TWO RACES IN THE SPRING OF 1981. THE FIRST WAS a race in mid-April to raise money for Chapel Hill students who would go overseas short-term that summer in Inter-Varsity's Student Training in Missions program. He came in second. The other race was at the Inter-Varsity executive planning retreat at Windy Gap. Every year at this retreat there is a road race for fun. Sandy had won the year before, but this year Billy Creech came in first. Sandy, lagging behind, had even stopped a couple of times as if he were out of shape.

As always, there was lots of laughter. And Debbie Bowers was there. Sandy was glad to be able to get to know her better. But most of their time was spent in Bible study, prayer and planning. They were asked to take their particular responsibility (Sandy was program chairman) and then dream, dream beyond the usual and normal. Sandy dreamed of an all-quad concert and speaker . . . a series of lectures on the university and Christianity . . . two hundred people at chapter meetings by next year . . . an evangelistic Bible study in each hall, twenty-five full-time Christian workers from the chapter in the next two years . . . a combined meeting of Inter-Varsity, Campus Crusade, Navigators and Maranatha (all campus Christian groups) to form a visible bond of unity. What Sandy could not have dreamed, nor anyone planned, was that some of these dreams would come true because Sandy was removed from the scene.

Sandy came back from Windy Gap to Debbie and Craig's wedding in May. This was the bright spot in a summer that was to be difficult and exhausting, particularly for Jeanie. Her mother was slowly dying. Mother Graham lived just two miles away, and Jeanie, who cared for her regularly, was emotionally worn from watching her die. Working on the wedding with Deb was a joyful distraction for Jeanie but an enormous amount of work too.

Apart from the wedding itself, the high point was probably the rehearsal dinner. This often stuffy affair was turned into a hilarious romp by Sandy. During the traditional roasting and toasting of the bride and groom, Sandy, who was usually so serious around home, had everyone aching from laughter. He described a family trip to Georgia when Deb demanded we stop every thirty minutes because she had swilled a soft drink just before we started. He advised Craig to plan a good rest stop before their honeymoon. Turning his assault to Craig, who is tall and athletic but not particularly muscular, he perfectly mimicked a crash course in muscle building in which Craig failed to produce a "line" on his biceps to impress Deb. He went on and on till everyone was breathless from laughing.

After a short break at the beach with Lisa Funderburk and her grandparents, Sandy headed north for Washington, D.C., to attend the C. S. Lewis Institute. He took a roundabout route to save on airfare and had a two-hour stopover in Atlanta. There he was surprised to see Mims Cook, a young businessman from Atlanta who had been at Deb and Craig's wedding but who mostly came to talk with Sandy about spiritual things. After their intense discussion at the airport, Sandy wrote that he felt Mims was "about to commit his life to the Lord." We learned later that, next to Mims's grandmother, Sandy had been the most powerful spiritual influence on his life.

The C. S. Lewis Institute was just what Sandy needed. He had two-year's accumulation of questions and doubts, arising from the university, from unbelievers in France, from his own questions about economics and evolution. He wanted to hammer out some answers in this intellectual forge and intended to make the most of his exposure to the Christian thinkers assembled there. His hopes were not disappointed.

At the institute Sandy also renewed friendship with Henry, a young man he had not seen in three years. Henry had been struggling spiritually. Jim Houston of Regent College, who was also there, observed the pair. Sandy treated him "as an equal, a close friend," Jim noted, "and therefore with no sign of patronizing. Sandy's humility was very evident with an unassuming spirit that took no advantage of his family heritage."

Wendy Magneson, Jim's secretary, also said, "The thing that impressed me most about Sandy was not his spirit, personality or Christian commitment, but the way he treated [Henry]. Sandy told me, in fact, that this other boy was *so* different from him, someone he found hard to relate to. Nevertheless, I saw Sandy stick by this boy that week and attempt to love him. Sandy was patient with him, though it cost him to do so."

From Washington Sandy flew to Canada to join me for a crusade in Charlottetown, Prince Edward Island. Graham Johnston, whom he had been with in France, was also coming, as was Ruthanne James, whose father, Homer, had sung at my crusades for years. The three of them were to help in the youth aspects of the crusade. The week on this emerald island—the locale for the well-known book *Anne of Green Gables*—was a delightful one in every way. Charlottetown is a small city full of long traditions, beautifully restored old homes and folk who have typical eastern Canadian reserve but warm hearts.

From the moment of arrival, Graham, Ruthanne and Sandy plunged into a week that overflowed with fun and challenges. They spoke at churches, helped in the crusade office, led an open-air Bible study for young people which grew from twenty-five to forty-five over the course of the week. They encouraged the young people to bring their friends to the nightly crusade meetings in the local hockey rink. Graham and Sandy alternated giving a brief challenge to the young people at the meetings, and almost every night there would be singing or some social activity afterward.

But there were also lots of opportunities for fun. One day some fishermen invited the whole team to their seaside home and served fresh steamed lobster. It was one of those unforgettable summer days in Canada—clear sky, warm sun, sparkling water. After romping with a playful local dog, Sandy, Graham and Ruthanne crowded into a two-seater convertible which had been loaned to them, and drove off, with shouts and waves, to the afternoon Bible study. Graham and Sandy agreed that even if they died then, they would have lived full and complete lives. "I had a fantastic time in Canada," Sandy wrote Lisa Funderburk, mentioning Graham but conveniently forgetting Ruthanne.

But things were not so cheery in Charlotte. Mother Graham's condition had deteriorated. She had not been strong enough to attend Deb and Craig's wedding and shortly after that had a very serious setback which put her in the hospital for some days. She rallied but never really recovered. By midsummer it was obvious that she was dying. Jeanie's fatigue was not helped when she sprained her ankle badly right after the wedding. With Mother Graham's health precarious, we could not get away for more than a few hours. Jeanie was wanting to rely on her elder son at just the time when, after an exhausting school year and a hectic spring, he most wanted to relax in the lazy days of summer. Sometimes family life got pretty tense.

The rest of that summer Sandy worked at Grier-Parker-Poe, a Charlotte law firm. A career in law, politics or international relations appealed to him and he had written to a family friend, Bill Poe, asking if they had an opening. Although it was rather unusual to take an undergraduate who was not a law student, they took him on as a general helper, sorting files and running errands— not particularly to his liking. He alternated between periods of intensely busy work and times when there seemed to be nothing to do. He came to admire many of the lawyers for the jobs they performed, and sympathized with some of the clerical help who seemed to be condemned to a "lifestyle which lives for coffee breaks and weekends." During the crusade in Charlottetown he had learned to soar. Now during the long hot summer he was plodding.

Still, the routine afforded opportunities to express his Christianity. One day when he had to do some paper shuffling to appear busy, he took time to buy a Coke for a black teen-ager who worked outside the office building and looked very hot. "Maybe he will feel like strangers even care," wrote Sandy. "I remember Jesus' words about giving a neighbor a glass of water. I really did it to Him."

During that summer he led a Bible class for a group of college students. Later another group at church planned two evenings which promised to be exciting. Jeanie suggested that he cancel the last two weeks of his Bible class to be with his friends. But Sandy said, "No, Mom. I made a commitment and I am going to stick with it."

On July 13, Sandy wrote to Lisa. He chatted about his Bible class, his reading of Richard Foster's *The Celebration of Discipline* and his work. "But as always the summer is going too quickly. In another month, I will be finishing work and heading back to C. Hill. I won't dwell on that. We Americans tend to be too future oriented and are always thinking or preparing for the next stage. Lisa, pray that I will live life each day."

The summer routine may have been a bit boring but it also provided a much-needed break. For the first time in a long while, he was able to take lots of time to run, play tennis and swim with his friends. "I enjoy being outdoors on a mild summer evening like tonight," he wrote on July 28, "especially swimming after the sun goes down. There is a rich summer flavor surrounding this." Although he was frustrated at not hearing from Lisa as much as he had hoped, he enjoyed hearing from his new interest—Debbie Bowers—and particularly enjoyed it when she came for a weekend.

Sandy had never related his feelings very freely, particularly at home. He tended to retreat within himself when he felt pressure, as he did this summer. I felt he was not being considerate of the stress Jeanie was going through. When I told him this, it hurt him far more than I knew. That night he wrote, "Tonight I am extremely frustrated. Dad tells me that Mom thinks that I dislike her. He told me at the dinner table that I would treat my wife like I treat her. It was another insult to me since they had both hinted before that I had treated Mom badly. This all hurts me so much that I can't even write about it any longer."

His hurt was no doubt due in part to the fact that he *had* tried to show his love for his mother. He was in Winston-Salem with

Billy Rice, Billy Creech and others for Fourth-of-July fireworks. Since the display ended about 10:00 P.M., Billy Rice asked Sandy to stay at his house overnight. The offer was tempting, especially with the prospect of goofing off with friends he hadn't seen in several weeks. But I was out of town and Jeanie was home alone. No, he thought it best to drive home that night. "I was impressed with his commitment to his mother," Billy Rice said.

Difficult times tend to force people apart or bring them together. Even Mother Graham's illness helped Sandy and Jeanie express their love more freely and to understand each other. They had some good conversations after that. A few days after I had talked to him, Sandy wrote, "It has been hard for me to express myself to Mom and to let her know that I really care for her at this time of emotional upheaval as we await Grandmother's death. She admits that she is hypersensitive. I pray that it will be easier for me to share with her her hurts, and also hope she will understand me more as I reach manhood."

Jeanie put it this way: "He was really involved in being a counselor and a discipler of other people, and I think as a result the family got shortchanged. Kevin and Deb and Leighton and me— we all got shortchanged. But I think he came home to receive and to be filled up, so he could go out and give. And that's the way it should be. But I think Sandy gave an awful lot more outside the home than he did inside the home. I just needed him more that summer."

While caring for Mother Graham and preparing ourselves emotionally for her death, we were quite unprepared for another shock. A dear friend, David Smith, an ophthalmologist and a sincere Christian, had been caught in a flash flood while tubing on a North Carolina mountain river. Darkness had halted the search for the night. With morning came bad news.

Sandy wrote, "Today I have had to face the reality of death. Dr. Smith's body was found. A small baby died at Lake Wylie right near the Belk's and we discussed some of Grandmother's funeral arrangements. Sometimes I get encased in my sugar-coated world and forget the sorrow and pain."

Several days later he went to his grandmother's house to see her for what he thought might be the last time. His Uncle Billy also stopped by. They talked about the timing of death. Billy cited Martin Luther King, Jr., and John F. Kennedy to illustrate how their premature deaths had made the impact of their lives even greater. He also pointed out that King Hezekiah, according to the Old Testament, had probably lived too long and undone much of the good that he had done earlier. The conversation impressed Sandy. That night he wrote that Uncle Billy stressed "that God takes each Christian at the perfect time—the time when He can choose to make the biggest impact."

With tensions high, Sandy and Kevin both wanted to go away for a weekend camping trip to the mountains. But after David Smith's death Jeanie and I were both fearful and overprotective. I persuaded them to change their plans and to take a weekend at the South Carolina beach instead. It would cost them more for a place to stay but I promised to subsidize that.

They found a room in a small hotel and swam, sunbathed and ate. "I think we packed a week's worth of activity into a day and a half," wrote Sandy.

The day after they got back, another minor escapade helped to bring the boys closer to each other and Sandy closer to Jeanie. Late that evening Kevin left the house twice and slipped off without anybody knowing where he was going. With the other pressures she was facing, and my being away at a conference in Kansas City, Jeanie was worried. Sandy told her he would look for Kevin, but he could not find him. He prayed for guidance.

Kevin returned sometime after midnight and Sandy questioned him, no doubt fearful that his younger brother was getting mixed up with drinking or drugs. Instead, Kevin told them that he had gone out by himself to find a place where he could chew tobacco, something he and his friends had been experimenting with! Sandy was relieved. The two of them had a good talk, and he encouraged Kevin to go kiss Mom good night. "Now I am finally relieved enough to go to sleep," he wrote at 12:42 A.M.

Big brother had another kind of message to deliver to younger brother two weeks later. Their grandmother finally passed into the presence of the Lord she had loved for so many years. One of the last moments that passed between her and Jeanie had come when Jeanie leaned over to kiss her. Mother Graham somehow raised her feeble arms, patted Jeanie on the shoulder, and said, "Pass it on to every generation." There was faith and love and hope to pass on, and when Sandy heard that she had died, he asked if he could be the one to break the news to Kevin. That night, he was again writing in his journal.

A saint died tonight! Grandmother has departed from her earthly body after eighty-nine and a half years and is now with our Lord Jesus—our hope.

Shortly after 7:00 P.M., Deb and Craig were at the house on Park Road and Grandmother took her last breaths. The news services had already imparted the news that, 'The mother of evangelist, Billy Graham, died tonight.' But this was in the world's eyes. From God's eyes I believe that . . . a saint joined a heavenly cloud of other saints and witnesses this evening.

I went in to see her body around 8:00. It wasn't her, it was an encasement. A worn, hard, crusty shell which housed an angelic spirit, beautiful as can be. It will be interesting to observe how this affects others in the family. I sincerely hope that it will bring us closer again—I mean the entire Graham family.

Tired and feeling a cold coming on, he prayed that the Lord would spare him during that tense and busy time. It seemed that he had a cold about that time every year. But he could hardly afford one now—with funeral preparations, as well as his imminent return to Chapel Hill.

"Yesterday we had Grandmother's funeral. It brought to me again the reality of death."

9
QUESTIONING FAITH

O*N THE UNIVERSITY OF NORTH CAROLINA CAMPUS AT CHAPEL HILL* there is an inconspicuous one-story building vaguely associated with computer science. Few people notice it. Even fewer know that behind this little building is a small garden guarded by tired brick walls, too high to see over, and a high vine-laden trellis. Under the trellis, a white patio table and chairs contrast with the dark red brick and greenery.

This was Sandy's favorite place to study. Here he could work without interruption, think and plan for large group Inter-Varsity meetings, and make notes for the next executive committee meeting. Sometimes he had his quiet time here. The red brick and the ivy-filtered light were more conducive to reflection than fluorescent tubes and confining study carrels. He'd told Billy Rice about it, but swore him to secrecy.

On this afternoon, early in March 1981, Sandy had been studying for Econ 32 and Poli Sci 41. Troubling stuff—jarring him out of his comfortable affluent environment. *How* does *a Christian respond to a world economy in which so few control so much, while the many in the Third World—why* Third *World?—have so little? Most of the Third World is non-White and non-Christian; many blame the "Christian" West for present injustice and economic "exploitation." Has the Christian Church messed up? What would a Christian international economy look like? What does all this mean for world evangelism and missions?*

Frowning, Sandy dismissed these thoughts for the moment and turned to a more practical task. As president of the Phi Eta Sigma honor society, he had to write his congratulations to the new members and give them details of the induction ceremony on the twenty-ninth.

Into the first paragraph, he wove this casual remark: "I want to encourage you onward in this pursuit of excellence. Personally, I feel that academic excellence, although not an end in itself, can prepare us to benefit humanity. It is a God-given tool of which we should be faithful stewards."

This thought, tucked neatly and unobtrusively into an otherwise perfunctory letter, expresses Sandy's forthright but gentlemanly way of joining faith and academics. He was a long way from completely integrating the two. But he was dealing honestly with questions and challenges to the Christian faith—and with his own doubts.

During his summer in France, Sandy's faith had been challenged as never before. Daily conversations with existentialists, Muslims and others stretched him intellectually. The same questions he was asked, he now began to ask himself. So he started to read about the rational defense of the faith and about the moral problems which face Christians.

This questioning was channeled in new directions by the classes Sandy took during his sophomore year, particularly economics and political science. By the end of the year Sandy had to declare a major. This further intensified his struggle to clear up what it meant to live out his faith in the world.

His sister, Debbie, tells it this way. "He was *out*wardly directed rather than *in*wardly directed. That's the one thing that made Sandy really unique in the generation that he was growing up in, a generation of apathetic people who didn't care, who didn't want to do anything and all they wanted was for themselves. Even a lot of Christians just want for themselves—want to have their neat little friendships and all their growth and all their whatever. Sandy saw what was going on in the world. He was interested in economics and politics. His eyes were very much outside of himself."

Jimmy Long, area director for Inter-Varsity Christian Fellowship in North Carolina, talked with Sandy several times that year.

"I remember our conversation in the pit of the student union. Sandy was struggling to choose an interdisciplinary major that would allow him to deal with economic issues, especially economic conditions in the Third World. He might even have wanted to work in a Third World country. He was looking at economics, political science and international relations insofar as they were related to economic conditions in the Third World.

"These conversations with Sandy are vivid because discussions on such topics were rare. The Christian community at Chapel Hill is large, and for most Christians life centers within the fellowship. People were not dealing much, at least in Inter-Varsity, with the moral issues of Christian involvement in the world, especially economic conditions. So I was pleased to see it in someone like Sandy. Where it stemmed from I'm not sure. He liked to read. I think he'd read Thom Hopler's *A World of Difference,* for example. And I think it was partly because of some of his classes that year. It wasn't just Christian influence, but influence from within the university.

"Then, too, Sandy was just other-oriented—he wasn't a narcissist. He was concerned about people. That's why he was concerned about the Third World, and for the same reason he struggled the year before about joining a fraternity, and in his sophomore year about whether to run for a student government office.

"Sandy was like most students at Chapel Hill—traditional, politically very conservative. But when they were exposed to issues of justice, they saw that as Christians they needed to be involved, that sometimes justice conflicts with traditional views of politics and economics. John Perkins from Voice of Calvary came to Chapel Hill to talk and I know Sandy heard him.

"But Sandy was far more open than most to taking classes that might conflict with what he believed. He was struggling with the whole question of justice and the Christian."

But questions of the moral integrity and application of his faith were not the only issues for Sandy that year. The people he met in France had doubted that the Christian faith was true at all. This question seemed to linger like a vapor about his sophomore year without ever dissolving the rock of his faith or impeding his activity in Inter-Varsity. He talked about these doubts with Richard Rhodes, an Inter-Varsity staff member at Chapel Hill who often ran with him. After one such talk (just before Christmas 1980) Sandy and Richard agreed to read Os Guinness's *In Two Minds* over the holiday. Sandy read the whole book that Christmas, and, when school resumed in January, he had resolved many of his doubts. Or so it seemed to Richard. But they were not to be so easily laid to rest.

He was still chewing on something too big to swallow when he left for the C. S. Lewis Institute in Washington, D.C., early in the summer of 1981. Closely alligned with Regent College of Vancouver, the Institute ran for three weeks immediately after school each spring. A wide selection of seminars were offered on topics related to Christian faith and principles, the aim being to help people think and live Christianly in every area of life.

The Institute provided Sandy with two things he very much needed—a relaxing break from pressure, and the stimulation of dialog with rigorously trained and thoroughly Christian minds. He wrote to Lisa, "This is what I have needed all year, a couple of weeks to read and renew myself." At the institute he met Charles Malik, the Lebanese statesman and former president of the UN, who gave a seminar on Augustine, and Klaus Bockmuehl, evangelical theologian, who taught a course on the Christian response to Marxism. From Bockmuehl he learned a critique of the basic materialism of both Marxism and capitalism and concluded that, from the biblical view, the widest possible distribution of private property was best. Jim Houston, a former Oxford geographer and Chancellor of Regent College, expounded the Beatitudes, while Nicholas Wolterstorff, a philosopher from Calvin College, introduced the various ways of defending the Christian faith.

Through his seminars he was coming to understand more about a Christian view of history, Marxism and public policy, and, as he wrote us, "to realize that Christianity is a part of everything, and to remember that God is involved with all of these aspects of life." He was still thinking about what he wanted to be in the future and suggested one option might be to finish his major in political science at UNC and then go to Oxford to work on an undergraduate major in philosophy. This would be followed by a seminary degree.

Jim Houston had been a good friend for a number of years. He remembered that Sandy's first concern on arrival had been to ask about evolution versus creation and what should be the Christian perspective. (About that time Sandy was reading *The Bible and Science Newsletter.*) They probed that issue quite deeply. They also discussed at length the matter of divorce among Christian leaders.

Sandy mentioned in confidence his concern about the divorce and prospective remarriage of a certain well-known Christian speaker that Inter-Varsity at Carolina had decided to invite. He had been in a small minority of the committee which had dissented on the invitation. "I assured him I held the same views," wrote Jim, "rather marveling that such a young Christian should be so wise and strong about such a stand."

Later that summer, Donny Little, one of Sandy's high-school friends, and Sandy met for lunch one day at Wendy's. Donny was astonished to hear Sandy—*Sandy!*—wondering aloud: What if the Christian faith is a big mistake? What if there is no resurrection? But Donny was reassured too by Sandy's openness because Donny had asked himself these same questions.

Not all of Sandy's questions and doubts were answered at the C. S. Lewis Institute. He was learning that questioning and doubt can stretch faith and not be antithetical to it.

When Sandy returned to Chapel Hill in the fall of 1981, he signed up for Professor Grant Wacker's course on religion in America. Taking this elective reflected his ongoing struggle with a number of issues. Like most religion courses in state schools, this class aimed to describe the various elements—social, philosophical, theological—that had contributed to the making of religion in America. It did not seek to prescribe what that religion should be.

"I did not know Sandy at all personally," said Professor Wacker. "I knew him only through his work—through two beautifully written midterm exams and a number of conversations after class. Sandy was an *A* student. As best as I could calculate, at the midterm, Sandy had the second-highest score in a class of about two hundred. But that's not all that important—we're not all cut out to be *A* students, and some *A* students are not very distinguished people.

"Sandy also had an unusual quality of discernment. It was evident that he saw through, he was extraordinarily perceptive. His observations were well-formed intellectually, and characterized by clarity and intelligence. But that too is an inborn gift, not entirely under our control.

"Sandy is a model—certainly for me as a teacher—in that he took the issues that were raised in that religion course with utmost seriousness. It was obvious Sandy was not taking that course merely to get a credit. And in a sense, it wasn't the course itself, but the issues, the problems he took seriously and wrestled with. That's what we talked about after class.

"Sandy was what I call a 'gentle' evangelical, not a 'militant' one. Evangelical Christianity would fare much better on secular campuses if there were more evangelical Christians like Sandy. He really cared about discerning the truth, wherever that might lead and however much that might hurt. My own perception of evangelicals—this is my own tradition—is that we are much too smug about our convictions. Sandy seemed convinced, but he certainly wasn't smug. Many evangelicals enroll in religion classes at secular universities as missionaries—they're going to convert their professor and the other students. They have not come to learn.

"G. K. Chesterton somewhere makes the comment that he became a Christian when he realized that Christianity did not tell the truth about this thing or that thing, but rather that Christianity was in itself a truth-telling thing. It seems to me that Sandy had something of that attitude. He saw it as both his obligation and his privilege as a Christian to wrestle through the problems of his faith as a truth-telling thing. I have been told that over the chapel at Andover Seminary in Massachusetts are engraved these words:

'To discern the true end in the great business of living.' Sandy's faith aimed at no less than that."

Sandy studied and reflected a great deal in that small walled garden in Chapel Hill. But his faith could not be contained there. He had begun to widen the scope of his faith so that all of life, transformed in its light, could be made good and beautiful.

10
A
GREAT
FALL

*A*FTER MOTHER GRAHAM'S FUNERAL, SANDY'S THROAT BECAME very sore. When it turned out to be strep, he put off leaving for Chapel Hill a day. A trip to Africa had been canceled for me, so the two of us had some unexpected time together in Charlotte. We talked about Sandy's future.

For some time, it had been obvious to me that Sandy's gifts and his heart were in ministry. His leadership, speaking ability, dedication, probing mind, faithfulness and desire to make a difference in the world convinced me of it. Jeanie and I had talked about this many times; she thought perhaps I should encourage him toward the ministry. I had never said anything to Sandy, though I had prayed about it, because I did not want him to feel pushed by me. Now I sensed the time was right.

I affirmed the gifts God had given him and the growth I had seen in him. He could make a contribution to the world and to the kingdom of God in politics, law, international relations or business, and he could do well in any of them. But I felt he was best suited to the ministry. There was no *greater* cause in which he could invest himself. Judging from his journal entry of the next day, these thoughts fell on a receptive mind.

> Last night Dad came right out and said that he thought it best if I invest my life in the ministry. He's never said anything like that until now. It's interesting that he would pick this time. Anyway, I've felt more drawn to seminary this summer even though I've been working at the law firm and admire many of them for the demanding jobs they perform.
>
> Oh yes, how can I forget. I received a letter from Lisa today. Isn't she thoughtful. She says she wants to see me in early Sept. I'm tempted to respond that I'll see her early next year. But maybe I'm being selfish and unfair. Who knows? Anyway, I've already received 2 letters from Debbie this week.

Stereo speakers were blasting from the sills of open windows. It was presemester party time when Sandy arrived at Chapel Hill. Sandy enjoyed the relaxed atmosphere as much as anyone, listening to live bands, mingling with friends he had not seen all summer. But after the very first Inter-Varsity event of the year—Fun Day—he was already struggling with what every leader faces: pride, the love of attention.

> Tonight I had several feelings of inadequacy. I'm not sure why. At Fun Day I felt that people didn't realize who I was, namely that I was a leader. I guess that isn't humility. Also, I feel that I should be involved in more things than I am. Mary and Dennis, for instance, are both RAs [Resident Assistants] and I am back here at Granville leading the same life. Perhaps the Lord will show me effective ways to be involved.

Finally, as I look around at all the couples here, I begin to desire that myself—a closer, more intimate relationship. Of course, the likely candidate now is Debbie B. However, I always think that there may be someone else there, once I start in a deeper relationship, whom I wish to know. Slowly, I'm beginning to give up on Lisa. Although she did write recently, I see no indication of real sentiment on her part.

I feel embarrassed about several of the things I've written tonight.

But he was soon thinking less about himself and more about an advanced French course and his religion in America course, both of which demanded a lot of time. Beyond course work, there were many Inter-Varsity activities: meeting with the exec on Sunday afternoon, putting up posters on Tuesday night for the Friday night meeting, and studying the Bible with a small group on another night.

He often went running all over Chapel Hill with Richard Rhodes while they talked about Inter-Varsity programs, about their spiritual lives or, just as often, about girls. Sandy was program coordinator for the Granville off-campus Inter-Varsity group. According to Richard, "Sandy had great vision for where the chapter should go—back to the basics. The Christian basics of the character of God, the gospel. And he and Billy [Creech] followed through with books for the rest of us to read." Sandy was amazed at the number of Christians on campus that fall and prayed that every individual would not treat their weekly meetings merely as social gatherings. There were *parties* for that.

One of the first planning meetings for the fall 1982 Billy Graham mission on campus left him both excited and nervous. Excited because he could see some of the dreams he had written at executive committee camp the previous spring becoming a reality. Nervous because of the responsibilities he would assume in preparation for the mission. As he thought about the year leading up to the mission, he believed "it to be important . . . for Christians to unite and begin praying for our hall."

Debbie Bowers was busy rushing sororities. But she had time to bake Sandy a pan of blueberry bread. This made his day, though he promptly forgot it. He and Freeman Broadwell, his roommate, found the remains of the bread weeks later—a mass of mold—and at arms' length threw it out. Some of the extra time he had was spent helping Debbie think through her sorority decision: whether to pledge and to which sorority. "I had gotten completely wrapped up in Inter-Varsity," Debbie said. "I thought joining a sorority would help me be in relationship with non-Inter-Varsity people. Sandy never alluded to his own decision about fraternities. He didn't burden me with his experience. He just asked me about my own needs and perspectives, and about what God was doing in my life and whether a sorority would help or hinder. When I joined KD [Kappa Delta], he sent me flowers."

Sandy's thoughts on the episode show him still to be a man in process. "I talked to Debbie on the phone and she had to cut three more sororities. Not one has dropped her yet. She didn't seem to be her cheerful self though. She is probably extremely weary after the whole process. I hope it is no reflection on me. Why do I always think like that? I always think that I may be burned, I guess. But this is where I need to continue to ask for self-confidence."

Labor Day weekend 1981 Sandy joined the whole family on Grandfather Mountain. We played tennis, went sailing on the lake—it was the best time we had had as a family in quite a while. After stuffing ourselves on country cooking at the Daniel Boone Inn, we laughed at the antics of Sandy, Kevin and Craig. That Saturday the boys and I hiked up to MacRae's Peak. The trail up the mountain culminates in a series of stout ladders tightly wired by the forest service to the rocks to make it possible to ascend some of the more precarious sections. At the summit is a huge boulder from which we could see for miles in every direction. There as usual we rested, had a chocolate bar and a drink, and said a prayer of thanksgiving before starting back.

Later that day, Sandy sat on the porch gazing up at Grandfather Mountain, washed in the rose tints of the setting sun. He had been reading and meditating on 2 Corinthians 6:14-18. There the apostle Paul calls Christians to be separate from the evils of the world. "What fellowship does light have with darkness?" As the sun set and the world turned further into the darkness, Sandy realized that he was sitting on the line between day and night. It was a moment when the truth of Scripture and the truth of nature combined to illuminate life.

> *2 Corinthians 6:14-18* What fellowship does light have with darkness? I sit on the horizon just when the sun has gone down. From here I can see the sun and its light, and those in darkness can still see me. I am like those horizontal clouds, red and luminous, reflecting the sun's light back to the darkness so that those who see them will have joy in knowing the light.
>
> Paul distinguishes here between the kingdom of Light and the kingdom of Darkness and sees them as mutually exclusive. Yet from the horizon I can fix one eye on the light and one eye on the darkness from where other souls come who wish to be saved.

Sandy did not share that insight with us. It was not his way. Nor, if he had, would we have realized then how like a cloud on the horizon at sunset his life was.

At family worship the next day, we discussed Ecclesiastes, the vanity and emptiness of life. Sandy's contribution was simple and direct: "I have come to see clearly the vanity of all systems which men build without God."

For all the personal inadequacies which Sandy felt, the central certainties were there. He knew what was the light of his life. He knew the difference between the kingdom of Light and the kingdom of Darkness. And he knew that his place was on the horizon.

September and October were extremely busy, full of the usual student routine plus Inter-Varsity responsibilities—leading planning meetings, and emceeing Inter-Varsity meetings with Dr. Ed Clowney and the *Habakkuk* multimedia show on campus. His academic load was heavy. In mid-September, Sandy wrote to Jeanie. He mentioned his studies, Inter-Varsity responsibilities and his intramural basketball team, the Sneezing Crocodiles. "If we win three more we will go to the finals." Then:

Last night before going to sleep I was looking through my journal and realized that I had written down a fair amount about you this summer. This summer I was able to get to know you better and I am glad about that. I think I have been making a transition over the past year or two from becoming your teen-aged boy to your grown-up son, of course, not fully grown up.

Before studying tonight, I dropped by Debbie's house to say hello. Perhaps that is why I studied so well! We are going out Friday night again. On Saturday night after the football game we went out to Bullock's in Durham. I was so excited about being with her, I could hardly concentrate on what I was doing. Anyway, we have been dating more and more; we have not talked about whether we will date other people or what. I know that I would like to at least see Christine and maybe Donna Dejong, but I already care so much for Debbie I am not sure if I should. What do you think?

Please pray for these things and know that I am praying for you.

Love,

Sandy

A few days later the Sneezing Crocodiles were defeated in the quarter finals. The defeat that usually would have rankled Sandy's competitive nature rated only a passing notice compared to the up-and-down state of his mind concerning his relationship with Debbie. "I am hesitant to give my heart away again in fear that I will be hurt. I sure can remember the pain after dating others. Yet I am seeking the Lord's will and know that I have to trust him. Whatever that may mean for Debbie and me."

Three days later he was up! "I really believe I may be falling in love with her. What a frighteningly exciting thought!" Even with this the need to be objective stuck with him. He wrote, "Isn't this silly—I could probably analyze the feelings of a rock if I tried."

Jeanie wrote back to say she was praying for every phase of his life including his relationship with Debbie. "If you care for her, you have to show it in little ways," she told him. She also hoped he could plan to come home for my fiftieth birthday, October 22. She was planning a surprise party.

He noted her suggestion and dropped by Debbie's sorority with a plant. He also began to wonder what he could do to surprise me for my fiftieth birthday. In one of the few journal entries written in French, he noted, *"Et j'ai commencé à écrire une poème pour papa parce qu'il a son cinquîeme anniversaire en Octobre."* (I have begun to write a poem for Dad because he has his fiftieth birthday in October.)

On Thursday the first of October, he went over to Peabody Hall quite late after studying and prayed and studied the Scriptures. He noted several things he felt the Lord was telling him.

"(1) That I needed to continue to seek him,

"(2) that it is necessary to be more willing to open up with the guys on the hall,

"(3) that I should appreciate and thank him for the way Debbie cares for me. It is a blessing from him at this point."

The semester was punctuated only by a relaxing weekend trip with Freeman Broadwell to his home in Asheville. They ate too many pancakes and porkchops, split wood for the winter, and concluded a discussion they had been having about the Jews—will they be saved or not? They decided that, according to Romans 9—11, they would be. A remnant of Israel, the natural branches, would be grafted back into the tree of God's plan.

When Sandy returned from the weekend in Asheville with his spirits high from mountain air and a break from routine, heartache replaced happiness. He went to see Debbie. She was quiet and told him she probably would not be able to go to the football game with him the next weekend. Hypersensitive, Sandy took this as a rejection. But the feelings did not last long. Sandy got down quickly, but he could get up again just as fast. On Monday night they had studied together. For some time, Debbie had been wanting to talk, and for a half-hour they spoke candidly about their relationship. "What a positive and assuring time!" he exulted. "After walking back," he continued, "I was wondering what I would have done if she had said she didn't want to date anymore. I thought I would probably be extremely upset, crying, and wish to pray. So, I thought I would go by Wesley Center and pray before going home and recognize God in good times as well as bad."

In the give and take of daily life and through the habits of years, members of a family seldom know accurately what other family members think of them. We often fail to let others know how we see them as whole persons. As parents, when we see our children begin to mature and set out on their own, we may feel unnecessary, perhaps even discarded. Yet, at just that time our children may begin to see us with new eyes and want to be proud of us.

As program chairman for the second semester of his sophomore year and the first of his junior year, Sandy had been hoping to arrange for me to address one of the all-quad meetings when the four Inter-Varsity chapters at the University of North Carolina came together. It was not his decision to make alone, however, and he felt awkward, thinking that as my son he should not push them to ask me. But the person they had originally wanted for October was set aside and, with real excitement, Sandy asked if I could come.

I flew in late that afternoon from the Boston airport just in time to make the meeting. Jeanie had driven up earlier from Charlotte. Sandy and Freeman picked me up and drove straight to the hall which was packed with several hundred eager Christians and their interested friends. He was disappointed not to get to introduce me. He sat with Jeanie and, in a demonstration of affection that was most unusual for him, kept his arm around her shoulders most of the time. Afterward, he stood with Jeanie and waited for Debbie to come to them. He always expected the girl to take this kind of initiative.

In preparation for the mission next year, the Inter-Varsity programs were being geared around basic Christian doctrines. Sandy and his committee had also planned the small group Bible studies that year to ground the Christians more firmly in these truths so they could present their faith intelligently to others. The theme Sandy had asked me to deal with that night was the spiritual lostness of people apart from Christ. I chose to do this by retelling three stories Jesus told: the lost sheep, the lost coin and the lost sons. In particular I zeroed in on the story of the younger son who left home and spent everything he had while the older brother stayed home and served his father but with a resentful heart. I pointed out that the younger son was searching for his identity but went about it the wrong way; the older brother was looking for security but searched for that in the wrong way. The younger son wanted his father's capital, the things that were coming to him, but not his father's control. And the older brother was willing to accept his father's laws, rules and regulations but knew nothing of love. Both sons were lost.

Sandy was impressed. "Tonight Dad brought one of the most

perceptive messages that I have ever heard. He spoke on the prodigal son, but he called it the lost sons. Each son was lost in a certain way and had different perceptions of the father. But the third son was in the shadows—it was Jesus who provided a right relationship with their father." About the three hundred fifty people who attended he said, "When he comes, it is always a little bit of an ego trip for me because everybody goes out of his/her way to speak with me. Perhaps this is just another advantage of being his son."

On September 29 Sandy had begun his poem for my fiftieth birthday. He had not completed it by October 22, however, and could not be at the surprise party Jeanie had planned; fall break ended and he had to return to Chapel Hill. Just before he left, he ran over to the shopping center and bought me a belt. Jeanie was disappointed, thinking that he took this milestone too lightly. But judging from the notes he made for the poem, this was not the case at all. Evidently, our talk about the ministry in late August was still on his mind.

You better with age (metaphor of wine in a gold cup)—compassion—uprightness—wisdom (aging mountains)—gentleness—model (mantle, 2 fold, Elijah). Like the wine, the violin and the mountains, yours is wisdom. A wisdom you have imparted to me, because I am you. Thus my prayer, like Elisha's, is to receive twice, when we part.

The first two weeks of November must have been an emotional firestorm for Sandy. So many good things were happening. He prepared for and wrote several important exams. On his religion exam Professor Grant Wacker had written urging him to come in and talk about doing graduate work in religion or theology. He had been asked to serve as the junior representative on the college honors council. He was thinking seriously about running for senior class president. Plans for the Billy Graham mission on campus for the next year were heating up and Sandy was on the steering committee.

Early in this same two weeks, Sandy ran into Susan Wheelon. They had not seen much of each other in a year and a half. "Sandy, we have just let each other down. We haven't had lunch. We hardly ever talk." Sandy laughed. It was the first time since their painful letting go that Susan had seen this casual joy in Sandy. He looked at her, and all of a sudden the choking feeling she had had around Sandy for months was gone. There was an unspoken understanding. They looked at each other like, "Boy, have we grown up!"

"We have got to get together for lunch," Susan said. "We have so much to share and I have so much to tell you. I know you are working on Billy Graham's lecture series, and I'm going to help in publicity, but I just wanted you to know the things the Lord has done in my life in the past year."

Since he had just put another major project behind him, he said, "I'd like to. We don't have any excuse."

They both laughed. "Sandy Ford, you have a good birthday. Isn't it next week?"

"I can't believe you remembered my birthday."

For the next ten minutes they went through a long list of "do you remembers." They laughed as the joy of their friendship returned. Sandy reached out and touched Susan's arm, "You take care and we'll get together for lunch. If not now, definitely after Thanksgiving."

She stood there and watched him walk away and said to herself, "I am going to hold you to that, Sandy Ford."

The first weekend in November, Sandy borrowed Richard Rhodes's apartment. He and Billy Creech had plans to cook dinner for Debbie and Sydney Hux. Shopping at Kroger's was a scene from a Laurel and Hardy comedy, especially for two guys who had never cooked a meal! (They were astounded at the cost of groceries.) Saturday, after the Clemson/UNC game, the girls, no doubt generously, said the meal was great.

But by the end of the second week of November, things were not so funny. One night Sandy burst into Billy Rice's room in Granville West. Extremely agitated and angry, he struck the wall: "What do you think about this?! Debbie and Danny are going to the beach together this weekend!" Debbie Bowers and Danny Harrell had been friends since the fifth grade. It had been a hectic semester, and they had not seen much of each other. So they checked with their parents and decided a weekend at the beach would be just the thing. Sandy and Danny had known each other since freshman year, but Sandy did not think it such a great idea. He was threatened and jealous; he could not see how they could go to the beach together for the weekend and just be friends. He told Debbie he thought it was a bad witness. Billy urged Sandy to call Danny and talk it over. But it was Danny who called Sandy. By then the trip was off, and Danny assured Sandy that he had no designs on Debbie. In the end, all three were reconciled and, by working through this crisis, Sandy and Debbie's relationship was better than ever.

The weekend of his twenty-first birthday saw a lot of things come together for Sandy. Visits from his brother and sister to Chapel Hill were rare. But he had dinner with Deb on Thursday and spent part of Saturday, his birthday, with Kevin, playing guitar and talking. That night he had dinner with Debbie Bowers. The next evening, the night of one of his first real preaching assignments at Moore's Chapel Baptist Church, he was selected to be president of the Granville-Off-Campus Inter-Varsity chapter starting in January. A big weekend indeed.

Dinner with his sister was full of conversation. Eventually she asked how his love life was going. Leaning forward, as he so often did, with elbows akimbo on the table, he nodded seriously and said, "Deb, I think that is just what it is." He was in love.

"Sandy said he wanted to marry somebody like me," Deb said later, "but he didn't want to marry somebody that was going to work. There was a lot about me that he liked, but I don't think he realized that a lot of it was wrapped up in being a motivated, career-oriented woman. He thought that a wife should do the laundry and the cooking and clean the house and do all the physical things that have been associated with women for years and years. I wasn't like that. We had a lot of arguments about it. He thought I was too liberal; I thought he was too much the chauvinist.

"He put a lot of energy into relationships. And he was easily hurt. He expected a lot of his girlfriends. I expected a lot of my boyfriends too. We grew up in a family where we knew what it was like to be in committed relationships. But we expected to have our freedom too. That's been hard for all of us. But Sandy was real insecure. If his girlfriend wasn't there when he called, he'd brood about it. He always wanted beautiful girlfriends. He always wondered how pretty or good-looking somebody was. That was one of the first things that he ever said about any girl that he dated."

Another friend, T. C. Collier, expressed similar thoughts. "As typical college juniors, Sandy and I were probably too concerned with looks. Yet two of Sandy's greatest assets were his love of beauty and his *joie de vivre,* and his concern with beauty and looks was never without a much greater concern for the heart. The mind is wonderful, but that in the end, it's the heart that energizes, gives life and matters."

Sandy loped easily alongside Freeman. Both wanted some exercise before supper. The roommates talked as they ran down Chapel Hill's oak-shaded streets, past the gracious old homes Sandy loved and yards blanketed with leathery brown leaves. Sandy's heart was as light as his feet—he would be studying with

Debbie Bowers later. After some push-ups and chin-ups at an elementary school playground, he and Freeman headed back to Granville West to shower.

After supper, they were back up in their room eating ice cream when suddenly Sandy looked scared and sat down on his bed. His heart had suddenly gone crazy. He felt very uncomfortable, peculiar, just as he had after basketball practice when he was fourteen. He told Freeman his heart was beating very fast and asked him to call an ambulance. Freeman did so and then ran for the hall paramedic, who was not in. When Freeman returned Sandy was lying on his back. While they waited for the ambulance, he told Freeman about the heart surgery six years earlier.

The wail of the siren and the flashing lights of the ambulance and the paramedics rushing up to fourth floor Granville West attracted great attention. The whole hall knew something was happening. Guys at open doors, or hurrying out of the elevator to make room for the stretcher with Sandy on it, were wide-eyed, concerned and curious.

"What happened to Sandy?" Few of them knew of Sandy's first operation.

"A heart attack?! How can you have a heart attack at his age— in *his* condition?!"

11
"BE GOOD
TO MY
BOY"

*I*T HAD BEEN A QUIET, UNDISTINGUISHED DAY AFTER WEEKS OF
hectic travel. Jeanie and I were enjoying an evening at home
together. We tried to call Sandy, but there was no answer. Kevin
was at a Young Life meeting. Jeanie was upstairs in her study
preparing for her Thursday morning Bible class when, shortly
after nine o'clock, the phone rang. A woman's voice. "Is this the
Ford residence?"

I identified myself. She continued.

"This is Dr. Brazeal from Memorial Hospital in Chapel Hill.
Your son Sandy has had a heart problem. He's here at Memorial."

Quickly and calmly she told me that Sandy had had a heart
arrhythmia which had lasted about forty minutes. He had conducted very rapidly and was converted back to normal through
electroshock. She assured me that he was all right, there was no

need for alarm, but they were keeping him under observation.

From her study, Jeanie could hear me murmuring questions. Her sensitive spirit knew immediately what had happened.

In the dead calm after the phone call, we were numb with disbelief. The peacefulness of the evening still surrounded us; the wave sent out from the dreadful shock Sandy had endured earlier that evening had not reached us until now. How could this be? Like a thunderclap on a clear day, the old nightmare was back.

We were still dazed when Kevin charged in from Young Life, threw his jacket on our bed and sat down to tell of the fun they'd had. Instead, we told him about Sandy. Then I called Deb; she burst into tears. I called Billy to ask for prayer. Jeanie and I talked briefly about driving up immediately, or the possibility of me driving up alone. But there was no point in that. We would leave in the morning. While Jeanie called to cancel her Bible class, I pulled the file on Sandy's operation, laid away and forgotten for six years. Déjà vu.

In a letter in the file the surgeon said the pathway in question had been divided and the life-threatening problem corrected. He did note, however, that there was evidence of still another pathway that could cause problems in the future. The future was all too present. But we tried to sleep.

The next morning, Thursday, Nov. 19, 1981, Kevin left for school and Jeanie and I for Chapel Hill. We did not talk much except to reminisce a bit about taking Sandy to Duke six years earlier. We went straight to Sandy's cubicle in the cardiac care unit at Memorial Hospital. The visiting hours for that area are very strict—ten minutes every several hours. But as Sandy was in no immediate danger, the nurses let us stay. Sandy was sitting on a chair, leaning over, elbows on his knees. One leg showed through a hole in his jeans. Jeanie ran her hands through his hair and said, "Hey, bud, what are you doing here?"

He looked up almost in tears and said, "I don't know." He was terribly frustrated, deeply upset about this problem recurring, but glad to see us. "Mom, why does this have to happen now? Everything was going so great!"

Then he told us what happened. He had run that afternoon, had done some sprints, followed by a good workout. Then he had showered and gone down for supper. He had ice cream for dessert. Back in his room, his heart had begun to beat rapidly. At first he dismissed it—it had happened before. He lay down on his bed, but his heart did not slow. Freeman was there and Sandy told him he needed help. When he saw that Sandy was having serious difficulty, he called for an ambulance and ran for the paramedic down the hall.

On the way to the hospital, Sandy tried to tell the medic team what the problem was, but they could do little to help. Finally, he was wheeled into the emergency room where they gave him a shot to relax him and applied the electric panels of the cardiac converter. His heart returned to a normal pace.

It was about noon when Dr. Parker, the head of the cardiology unit, came to talk with us. Without a doubt, Sandy had had another arrhythmia from the WPW syndrome. He tried to reassure us: advances had been made since Sandy's surgery six years before. Mapping and surgical techniques had been improved. New medications were available. He had put in a call for Dr. Gallagher at Duke, but John was in Dallas at the Heart Association and would not be back until late that night.

"Doctor, I'm really frustrated that this has happened at the end of the semester. I don't want to lose all my credits. Do you think I could go back to my classes and finish out the semester and *then* take whatever testing there has to be?" Dr. Parker would not commit himself on this.

"Then how about letting me out of this cardiac unit?" Sandy asked. "It's so depressing in here."

Parker explained that they had to monitor his heart and there was no other room available on the floor. He would have to stay there at least another night.

But Sandy's windowless cubicle suddenly became cheery with the arrival of some friends. His face lit up. I slipped out to get some of his textbooks at Granville West. When I arrived, the guys gathered in the hall to hear what news we had of Sandy. On the wall of his room was a poster. "I was born not to pass judgment, but to love." And pinned to his bulletin board, in his own hand was this: "For our light and momentary troubles are achieving for us an eternal glory that far outweighs them all. So we fix our eyes not on what is seen, but on what is unseen. For what is seen is temporary, but what is unseen is eternal. II Cor. 4:17, 18." I collected his things, returned to the hospital, and then we left him for the night.

That night and the next morning we went back and forth over the possibilities. If Sandy had to have some tests—and if the possibility of another surgery was entertained—it might be best to go ahead and get that out of the way right now. The school officials were sympathetic when I called. Sandy could postpone his exams and take an incomplete on his courses until January. Already we were beginning to look at the bright side. It was good that the attack came at the end of the semester when his courses were almost through; good also that they got an EKG on him while his heart was going so rapidly. After the previous surgery, Dr. Gallagher had said it would be ideal to get an EKG while his heart was under stress so they could do the most accurate analysis possible.

But Sandy was not looking on the bright side. "I am scared of what I may have to face in terms of tests or an operation. In fact," he wrote in his journal, "I am really very angry that it happened again. Haven't I had my fair share or more of that?" On Friday the other rooms on the floor were full again. Sandy would have to spend another night in his cell. Friday morning Jeanie opened the door to leave the cardiac unit, and there was Debbie Bowers, looking utterly bewildered, scared. She had been there a while, not knowing what to do. In an instant, Sandy's whole demeanor changed. He was delighted. His journal showed it.

"Although I cry to the Lord and I don't hear him, he is coming to me through my many loving friends. What a delight to see how people care! Debbie came by this morning and was so cheerful and understanding. . . . Already these moments have seemed to make our relationship much closer and deeper. . . . Finally, I am understanding how much she does care for me."

Cheered by Debbie's presence, Sandy was able to think constructively. In order to cover his courses that afternoon, I offered to go to his religion class for him. He was drawing a map for me when Dr. Parker came in.

A sea change showed in his face. He had talked with John Gallagher. They agreed that Sandy's attack was extremely serious, as serious as the one six years before. They could not allow Sandy out of the hospital for he must be monitored and close to instant care. If Sandy had another attack, it could be fatal.

We said nothing. He continued. As for medication, based on Sandy's previous history, conventional drugs probably would not work. Three or four experimental drugs were being used in Europe and South America, but all had side effects. If they tried them, Sandy would have to stay in the hospital—maybe for months. If surgery was the choice, on the other hand, then it would be best to transfer Sandy to Duke for testing.

When he left, we sat quietly with our thoughts. Six years ago— a sabbath cycle—arrhythmia, WPW, tubes, needles, endless hours of cath tests, the everlasting wait of surgery. Gallagher's smile, thumbs up, "Welcome Home, Sandy!!" Czar, running, studies. My son! growing in wisdom and stature. Now this life-threatening beast slinks out again. Why now? Thanksgiving!

Finally, Sandy said, "I feel trapped." And so did we. In his journal he wrote:

> Today has been a day of much stress emotionally; both good and bad. I am trapped between two unfortunate options. . . . I've cried along with Mom and Dad today and we all are torn inside with anger and confusion. . . . As I call out to the Lord, "Why?" it seems as though he has forgotten me. I feel boxed in, but know that if I learn to allow the Lord to carry me in this situation and learn to soar as a free eagle, then after this struggle when I am set free, I'll be a much greater witness for him. . . . I pray to God that he will heal me and restore me to perfect health, and I pray he will soothe any bitterness on the part of Mom and Dad.

I walked out of Sandy's cubicle to make a phone call. As I hung up a young man wearing a green orderly suit limped past me. He turned, looked at me strangely for a moment and said, "Dr. Ford?"

The face and the limp were familiar. Where had I seen him? In a hospital? Where? Here! Six years ago. I was reliving a nightmare! Steve Pleasants had been a patient at Duke when Sandy was. He had been through a bad car wreck which had left him with that permanent limp.

"Steve! What are you doing here?" I asked stupidly.

"I *work* here. What are *you* doing here?"

I pointed over to Sandy's cubicle. "Sandy's in there."

Disbelief was on his face as he walked in to talk to Sandy. A weird feeling came over me. Was there a wheel of fate after all which kept turning and which had caught us up again, perhaps to crush us?

But there was no time to be philosophical. When I called John Gallagher, he confirmed what his colleague had said. And if surgery was contemplated, it would have to be one of the next two Fridays because of Dr. Sealy's schedule. I told him we were still debating the surgery, but in the meantime we would arrange to move Sandy over to Duke. Dr. Gallagher was to meet with us there on Saturday afternoon.

It was a long day and a long evening. We were confused, frustrated and resentful. It helped Sandy to have some of his friends stop in. Jeanie and I worked off some of our frustration arranging for the move and for Deb and Kevin to come up the next day. I called an associate on the phone to tell him what was happening. Almost as an afterthought, I asked Irv if we could get two or three tickets for the Duke/Carolina football game the next afternoon, just in case Deb and Kevin might want to go when they came up.

On Saturday morning, Sandy stopped by his room at Granville and saw Billy Rice for a minute. After a walk with Debbie Bowers, Sandy was ready for the fifteen-mile trip to Durham. Sandy wanted to drive, so we let him. At the new Duke Medical Center, he was nervous and quiet. He wanted to handle as much of the admission procedure as possible. He was frustrated when I had to supply some insurance information. Feeling trapped, he needed to exert control.

The tickets to the Carolina game came through. If Sandy could go, I figured it would cheer him up. But how to get him there? Once he got up to his room on the eighth floor, I guessed they would put a monitor on him and would not let him leave. And I was sure if he asked permission of the doctors, they would not take the responsibility for letting him go.

"Why don't we get a bite of lunch down here in the hospital cafeteria before we go up? Jeanie, why don't you and Sandy go in and I'll take Sandy's things up and then come down and join you." After lunch, I suggested to Jeanie that she go up to Sandy's room while he and I walked. Aside, I quietly slipped her one of the tickets and told her to give it to Kevin when he came. The stadium was only a short walk away. We agreed that I would call every fifteen minutes. When Dr. Gallagher showed up, we would come back immediately.

"Come on, Sandy, we're going for a walk."

"Where are we going?" he asked glumly. I could see that a walk was the last thing on his mind.

"You and I are going to see Carolina beat Duke."

He looked at me incredulously. I held up two tickets.

"You're crazy!" he said. "We can't do that!" And he began to laugh.

"Listen, bud, we're going to beat the system. We can come back any time, but we're going to see part of that game."

We had taken so many father and son walks together—down Glen Falls in the North Carolina mountains; up Mt. Debar with Kevin in upper New York state; through the woods behind our house in the snow, pausing to watch two startled foxes run from us. On that cold clear November day, we crossed the Duke campus, got lost in the basement of the Divinity building, and passed through the lovely quadrangle, on walks littered with red dogwood leaves, to the stadium. We talked about how he was feeling, how scared he was that there might be surgery. I asked him how he felt when he was having the attack on Wednesday night.

"I was scared, Dad, really scared. I knew that I might be dying. I thought a lot about my friends. I thought about the work I had to do."

We talked about how strange it is that as Christians we know that we are going to be with the Lord, and we know that it is going to be better, but we are not quite ready to go there yet. Unlike Paul, who wrote to the Christians at Philippi that he wanted to depart and to be with Christ, to us life is beautiful. Life is sweet, especially when you're twenty-one.

When we got to Wallace Wade Stadium, a roar went up. Carolina had just scored. We were checking our tickets to find our section when we heard, "Dad! San!" It was Kevin. He and Sandy embraced. I sent the guys down to our seats, and went for a phone. Gallagher had not yet showed.

Down on the field, Carolina, inspired by their great running back, was taking the game from Duke. But Duke was fighting. The game was close and exciting. But by the end of the third quarter, Sandy had had enough. A brisk wind had come up, and he did not want to risk a cold if he had to go to the cath lab for tests on Monday.

John Gallagher showed up at 4:30 and for the next three and a half hours reviewed the entire situation with us. John's hypothesis was that during the first surgery, they had not completely severed Sandy's errant pathway. The path that remained intact had been bruised so that temporarily it did not conduct. That would account for the inability to make his heart beat rapidly when they tested him after surgery—a bruised electrical conduit will not conduct impulses; it would also account for some of the subsequent episodes of flutter—the bruised pathway had mended. Moreover, he now was certain that both of Sandy's surplus electrical circuits—not just one—were capable of conducting.

John stood for the first hour, then sat on Sandy's bed. Sandy sat crosslegged on the bed. Occasionally he would go over to his food tray, pick up the lid, just look at the food and put the lid back down. Jeanie, Deb, Kevin and I were on the sidelines, asking a few questions. Hour followed hour. I could not believe he was giving us so much time. He seemed to feel some special bond to Sandy.

All the drugs they might try instead of surgery had problems. One—Amiodarone—could turn the skin gray, affect the thyroid and alter the cornea. Surgical procedures had improved since Sandy's first attack. They had now operated successfully in the septal area at the rear of the heart where Sandy's two errant pathways were.

"In sum, surgery is my recommendation. Dr. Sealy could do it next Friday or the Friday following." Surgery seemed all but certain.

The next hour and a half were probably the hardest of my life. I was scheduled to preach at First Presbyterian Church in Winston-Salem for the next two days—Sunday and Monday. As I said good-by, I wanted to tell Sandy I loved him, but emotionally I couldn't. I was barely on the road headed to I-85 when it suddenly hit me that I was all alone. I started to cry—great heaving, pulsing sobs that almost pulled my insides out. Blinded by tears, I had to pull over and stop.

I could not believe this was happening. Why must my son go through this again? Why must he face surgery? And why *now*? This was the best time of his life. Everything was going great. The week before, he had been elected president of his Inter-Varsity Christian Fellowship chapter. That very week, he had been invited to be a junior member of the Honors Advisory Council. His religion professor had encouraged him to do graduate work in religion or theology. He was in love. Why did he have to go through this now? Why do *we* have to go through this? It just was not fair. I resented it and I was angry.

But most of all, deep in my heart there was a terrible fear, a fear that I did not, could not voice to anyone: what if this time the surgery did not work? What if this time Sandy should die? On that late, lonely drive to Winston-Salem, I cried to the Lord out of the depths. Did he hear me?

That Sunday morning, Sandy's Uncle Billy and Billy's daughter Anne stopped to see Sandy on their way home from New York. Sandy told them honestly that he thought it was unfair for him to be in the hospital again. It was unfair for Joseph to be in prison for thirteen years, Anne pointed out, especially when he had committed no crime. But God used that to prepare him for future leadership. "Anne reminded me of one of the psalms," Sandy wrote in his journal, "in which David was trapped and could do nothing himself. It is at this point, she said, that God is able to fill you (me) with his Holy Spirit." Jeanie and Debbie Bowers were there also. It was a sweet and supportive time for Sandy.

Suddenly the door flew open and there, out of breath, sweating, stood Lisa Funderburk. She had obviously been running though she was dressed for church. For a moment no one said anything; Lisa was unprepared to meet Billy, Anne and Debbie there; and they did not know what to make of her panting presence. Things were made even more delicate in that Lisa and Debbie had never met.

Lisa had been at Blacknall Presbyterian Church. She had not dated or talked to Sandy in some time, and was unaware of his attack and hospitalization. So when someone stood and requested prayer for Sandy Ford who was facing possible surgery, it came almost as a physical blow. Hardly knowing what she was doing, she rose, left the church and ran about a mile to the hospital. Things had gone sour between these old friends and sometime sweethearts largely because of a lack of communication. On July 20, a week after sending his last letter to Lisa, Sandy had recorded his frustration in his journal: "I am getting irritated that I have sent five letters to Lisa and have received one. This is worse than last summer. I am fed up with this game she plays. Let's count it her loss, if I can be so modest."

Lisa was not a good correspondent, but she was not playing games either. Sandy was so objective and businesslike in his communication that Lisa was not sure what Sandy wanted. But since she knew she was going to heaven because of Sandy, she also knew something had to be done about this estrangement. She must talk to Sandy and set things right between them. But obviously, this was not the time or the place. Having made brief contact and expressed her concern to Sandy, she left the hospital. The look in Sandy's eyes had given her what she needed: It's O.K. We're still friends.

Meanwhile, in Winston-Salem, God was moving the staid

members of the First Presbyterian church to walking the aisle in repentance and rededication. I told them about Sandy and about my struggle with God and about the hope of the gospel. Pastor David Burr is a man of prayer. Between services on Sunday he told me he had been praying the week before about these services and had had an intuition that I would be able to come only on Sunday, not for Monday. He released me from my obligation, and I returned to Durham Sunday night. Before leaving, though, I called Sandy.

"Sandy," I said, "when I left last night and we hugged and you told me you loved me, I wanted to tell you that I loved you too. But I couldn't. I was just overcome. But I wanted to explain."

"I understand, Dad," he said. And I knew he did. "And, Dad, don't try to come tonight. You'll be too tired, and I want to get some sleep to be ready for the cath labs tomorrow."

While I was driving back from Winston-Salem, Sandy had some effervescent visitors, among them his prayer partner at UNC, Mary Maddrey.

"Billy Creech, Eddie Wilson, Serena Harrell, and I went over to Durham after the executive meeting," Mary told us. "But we got lost. To keep our spirits up, Serena and I sang to Billy and Eddie. We were quite silly by the time we saw Sandy. It was pretty late, but the nursing staff let us stay. Serena and I sang a song entitled 'Sandy' from the movie *Grease*. Had I known then what I know now, I wouldn't have sung it. The words go 'in heaven forever and ever we will be, so please say you'll stay, oh Sandy.' We were trying to make him laugh, and he did crack a smile, but he said that he wanted to talk to us seriously for a few minutes. He said that God was showing him the importance of suffering for his name's sake. To be more like Christ, he too was having to suffer. He told us how this was going to have an effect on the campus. He asked us to pray with him. But before we did, we sang more songs and joined arms. I prayed first and I began to cry. I just hurt

— 152 —

all over. Then Billy began to cry as he prayed. Sandy didn't even say anything, and he cried with us. But it was a sweet love we all shared."

"We act like this when there is a crisis," Sandy had exhorted them. "But this is the way God wants us to be all the time, really caring for each other whether there is an emergency or not. God has been speaking to me about that."

The next night, in the calm of watching football with Billy Creech and Freeman Broadwell, Sandy made the same point. We should care for each other even when it's not a crisis.

Six years before, the cath tests were the hardest part of the ordeal for Sandy. This time the tests were not as long. "Mom, that wasn't so bad," Sandy told Jeanie over and over. Testing had been improved so that they were able to get four times as much information in less time. The tests confirmed Gallagher's hypothesis. Sandy indeed had two extra pathways. As Gallagher put it, "They probably talked to each other." One set the other off when the abnormal rhythm occurred. The tests seemed also to confirm that one pathway was on the left, the other on the right. Things seemed to be under control. We were relieved, thankful and cheerful.

We had been neglecting things in Charlotte for almost a week. So on Tuesday, I drove back home to see Kevin, get some more clothes, go to the bank, pay bills and look after other mundane details. Jeanie stayed with Sandy. I did not want to leave him because I still feared inside me that he might die—these might be the last days I could spend with my son. On the way, I listened to some Christian radio programs. One of the preachers was coming on strongly that God always wants his children to have health, hope and happiness. I wondered.

Back at the hospital Jeanie was with Sandy. He played the guitar and sang some new songs he was learning for her. Sandy discussed what he was learning about Kierkegaard, Barth and Bonhoeffer, being a bit amused that Jeanie even recognized the names.

That evening, when it was time for Jeanie to leave, Sandy said, "Mom, where are you parked?"

Jeanie pointed out the window. "It's not in the lot but on that side street."

It was dark and the car was quite a ways from the hospital. "Mom, don't ever park there again. That really bothers me. I'll stand in the window and watch you as far as I can. Then when you get back, call me and just let me know you're O.K." Jeanie did as requested.

I was busy in Charlotte until the next day when I met Kevin for lunch. He was excited about running for his class executive council, and had given his speech just that morning.

"I think it went well, Dad. Lots of people said it was the best speech, but I really don't think I'll get elected." He had closed his speech with a brief prayer which some thought stupid and some had appreciated.

That afternoon just as I was preparing to leave the house for the trip back to Duke the phone rang. It was Kevin.

"Dad, I made it!" he exclaimed. "I've been elected to the executive council!" He was thrilled. I told him Sandy would be excited and proud also. On that thankful note I headed back to Durham.

Sandy had so many visitors on Wednesday that Jeanie had been unable to spend much time with him. As one of those many friends left, Sandy alluded to the surgery. "I sure hope nothing happens on that table."

That evening, when John Gallagher came to review the results of the cath tests with us, he was optimistic. "We know where the pathways are, and we are almost positive we can get them." We also discussed at length the remote possibility that Sandy might need a pacemaker if the operation was not completely successful. A pacemaker would certainly be better than Sandy being in danger the rest of his life.

Jeanie and I left Sandy early that evening and went to dinner at Darryl's. The next day would be Thanksgiving. We would not be together as a family, and we were feeling it. Deb would be with Craig in Charlotte; Kevin was at a Young Life conference at Windy Gap for the weekend. Over dinner we did our best to be reconciled to the circumstances: we went over all the "what ifs"—things could be worse. All in all, if Sandy had to have an attack, this might be the best possible time. We prayed together, giving thanks as best we could.

Alone at the hospital, writing in his journal, Sandy was making his own peace.

I believe the Lord is showing me some of life's true perspectives and forcing me to cherish the blessings I so often take for granted. Yet I don't want to pretend to have all of the answers and reasons why I am going through this. But I know one is that we are imperfect and we are fallen.

Last night I was asking Debbie how she would perceive me and how others would perceive me if I did have an artificial part planted in me like a pacemaker. She reminded me that our society places great emphasis on being glamorous and perfect, but . . . to the ones that really loved me, it wouldn't matter. Although I wouldn't want a pacemaker I am beginning to think that I could accept it if the Lord wills it.

That Thanksgiving morning we were scheduled for a conference with Dr. Sealy. He was his usual businesslike, reserved self. But what he said toppled the peace we had so delicately balanced the night before.

The operation was going to be much more difficult than the first time, especially going for the pathway on the right. Scar tissue from the previous operation might have obliterated familiar land-marks, making it difficult if not impossible for him to locate the errant pathways. We all thought the obvious; Sandy expressed it: if they had not cut the pathway the first time, then it seemed there was even less chance that they would locate it and cut it this time.

Dr. Sealy indicated somberly that this was a real possibility. We had not realized until then just how difficult the surgery would be. He was optimistic, however. They would not be going in, he said, if they did not think they could get it.

Sandy asked about a new surgical method we had heard about that would make the scar less visible. The scar from the first operation had always been a great embarrassment to him. But Sealy would not commit himself to using this method.

When Dr. Sealy left, my mind was awhirl with new complex-ities. Just that morning he had told us about an abnormality in Sandy's A-V node, the amazing little device which regulates the electrical impulses to the heart. It was the first we had heard of this. And now a new uncertainty occurred to us, one too unset-tling to talk about. What if they were unable to solve the problem? Could they know for sure whether or not they had cut the extra pathways? Would Sandy have to live for years never knowing whether some random, unforeseeable and unavoidable event would again touch the hair trigger of his heart? To endure all the pain, the uncertainty of surgery and accomplish nothing—that was too much. Sandy was depressed.

I called Dr. Gallagher and told him the situation. He said he would try to get over to see Sandy that afternoon. Dr. Sealy, he went on, was probably reacting to a recent difficult surgery. It was a second surgery, and when they opened her up, the scar tissue was so bad, Sealy groaned, "My God! There is nothing I can do!" But in fact, the surgery was successful because of a new freezing technique.

We stayed with Sandy until he had eaten his Thanksgiving

dinner. The food was good at Duke, and he ate everything—he was afraid he was losing weight—he was down to one hundred and thirty-nine pounds. Then we drove to Chapel Hill to have Thanksgiving dinner with the Spences. While Jeanie napped before dinner, I went for a run on the campus. My heart was heavy as I pounded over Sandy's familiar ground. Overlooking one of the playing fields, I stopped, hunched down and wrestled with God. *You can heal him, I know you can. For what reason would you not heal him? Why wouldn't you heal my son?* I wept. People walked by; I tried to hide my face. *If you wouldn't heal my son, you must be something different from what I've always imagined. Are you? Are you?* With scalding tears, I prayed the only prayer I knew how to pray. *God, please be good to my boy tomorrow. Please be good to my boy!*

Thanksgiving dinner was a pleasant interlude, relaxing with friends. But by four o'clock we were back at the hospital. We watched football with Sandy, paged through a magazine or two, talked aimlessly. Deb and Kevin had called to talk to Sandy; Deb was coming up tomorrow, rather than waiting till Saturday. Other friends had called too. And Dr. Gallagher had stopped in for a long talk. One of Dr. Sealy's assistants arrived while we were there with a form to be signed giving permission for surgery. Sandy had just turned twenty-one, so he signed it himself. That and Dr. Gallagher's visit gave him a sense of control—he was an adult in charge of his own life.

About six, Debbie Bowers showed up. She had been with her family for Thanksgiving. She had told Sandy she would try to get away to visit him before the operation, but he had not counted on her. Now his face lit up as she entered the room. We left them alone; Jeanie had discovered that it was best to leave when his friends came.

Later, David Spence came. While he visited Sandy, we took Debbie out to dinner. We wanted to get to know her. But she wanted to know more about Sandy. What he did in high school, how he and Kevin fought, what he liked, who his friends were. She was in love. And we loved her because her love and presence were such a joy to Sandy.

Sandy was to be awakened at 6:15 the next morning to prepare for the operation. So we all prayed with him and left early.

While we were getting ready for bed, Sandy was preparing for the ordeal ahead. He took the phone off the hook to get some quiet to read his Bible and pray. His prayer partner, Mary Maddrey, tried several times to call him, but his line was always busy. About 11:30 P.M. she tried one more time and Sandy answered. He told why his line had been busy. "I'm a little anxious about tomorrow. But I'm ready for whatever the Lord wants from me."

At the Hilton—the same Hilton we stayed in six years before— I remembered how we had prayed then too, and the passage from Hosea we had read. I suggested to Jeanie that she sleep in because it would be a long day. But she insisted. She wanted to go over early to see Sandy before they took him. Knowing that friends were praying and that Sandy was in God's hands, we set the alarm and slept.

The alarm goes off at 5:45. With hardly a word, we get up and dress quickly. Ours is the only car in the circle at the hospital; all is quiet. Sandy is awake and appears to be rested.

"You seem calm."

"On the outside, Mom, not inside."

They have already given him Valium and perhaps Demerol. We ask questions, he replies. Mostly, he lies there peacefully. We wait. Jeanie can't stand the tension. She gets up and starts to straighten the room which is cluttered with cards and Sandy's things.

"Mom, please don't do that now."

It's 6:45. 7:00. They should have come for him at 6:30. We hear a sound—they're coming for him. But no, it's just another cart. We wait; we pray with him; we read Scripture. Wait some more. Waiting. Absently, Jeanie again begins to straighten his room. Again, he stops her.

"Mom, you know they shaved me from my chest to my knees." He is embarrassed by this.

Finally, at 7:15, they come. Very quickly, they move him from the bed to the cart. They take off his new warm flannel pajama bottoms he has liked so well—his legs have been cold—and transfer his IV to the cart. Jeanie says for me to go with him and she will stay here.

"Bye, Buddy, I love you."

"Bye, Mom. I love you too."

We start down the hall. I have to walk quickly to keep up. We get on the elevator. Two or three attendants and the nurse chatter away. At the entrance to the operating room, I hesitate. The attendant sees me, smiles, waves me in. Dr. Karis, the anesthesiologist, the same one who worked on Sandy six years ago, checks him over, asks how he is.

To me, he says, "We'll take good care of him." I say something. I reach out and grasp Sandy's hand. I smile. He says something. I mumble, "See you later." And he's gone.

When I return, Jeanie shows me a card she found on Sandy's bed. On it are the words of Psalm 73:21-26. "My flesh and my heart may fail, but God is the strength of my heart and my portion forever." Apparently a friend gave it to Sandy last night for him to meditate on.

Jeanie and I go back to the Hilton to get some more sleep. At 8:30 a phone call from Billie Barrows wakes us. Preston Parrish, of my team, joins us for breakfast, and Jeanie finds it difficult to talk with anyone else—even good friends. Breakfast over, she returns to our room while Preston and I go to the hospital and move Sandy's things to 3110, the room Dr. Sealy reserved for him on the third floor. Since it is Thanksgiving weekend, there is little surgery scheduled and the floor is nearly empty. Preston stays at the hospital while I return for Jeanie.

The night before, when David Spence came to the hospital, Sandy told him that through all this God was giving him a new sense of priorities. When he gets out he wants to spend more time with his non-Christian friends. David feels that, having had so comparatively ideal an upbringing, Sandy is now learning much about the grace of God in times of need—something he would never know were he never tested in this way. He will be deeper and stronger, David feels, because of it. I remember Sandy wondering whether his faith was just a function of his home environment. He's finding out now.

Around noon, Deb calls from the hospital. She and Irv have just arrived from Charlotte. Jeanie and I leave the Hilton and join them in 3110. Conscious that Sandy is in surgery, we talk about other things. Twice I walk down and stand by the doors of the operating room. Only a few yards away is my son. I send my prayers through the wall.

One o'clock comes and we decide to get something to eat. Preston, Irv and I go first. When we return, Jeanie and Deb go. At 2:00 I take Irv and Preston for a walk. We go over to the old Duke Hospital and I show them the chapel. Then I go back up to Jeanie and Deb. We wait. Between 2:30 and 3:00 Debbie Bowers comes to wait with us. She expected that we would have some word by now.

Anticipation begins to set in. We have had no word all day. Dr. Sealy said the operation would take between three and a half to seven hours. They started between 8:00 and 8:30, they should have been through at the earliest by 11:30, at the latest by 3:30. During the first operation, we were informed every two hours. Surely some word will be coming.

Finally, about 2:50 the first message comes—they have found and severed the first pathway, they know where the second one is and they are going to work on it now. It will take another hour and a half to two hours. We estimate that about 4:30 or so they will be finished and Sandy should be in recovery. We ask them to please keep us informed.

Joe Greer, a friend who worked in the hospital, comes to see us and we ask him if he knows anything. He goes and comes back. Sandy is already in the recovery room! Our hearts lift—its over! They've fixed his heart! But when he returns again, he has made a mistake. The chart simply shows where Sandy will be when he is through the surgery.

It is getting close to 4:30. They promised to have further word by 3:30. I ask another nurse. She checks and says they still have a few problems or something to that effect. We really begin to be concerned. 5:00. 5:15. We sit in the room, waiting, waiting.

I try to read the *Time* cover story "Paradise Lost," but there is no way to concentrate. I walk up and down the halls, Jeanie encourages me to take another walk, but I can't do it. I have to be here. Any moment they may come; any moment we may get a call. 5:30. Surgery started at 8:15. It has been nine hours—two hours over what Dr. Sealy suggested. How long can he be on the heart-lung machine? How long can they operate? They have spoken of problems. There must be something more than we anticipated.

One of the nurses comes in again, apologizes for the lack of information, explains that no one should have said there were problems. Period. She leaves us teetering over world-swallowing abysses of our imagination—what is wrong? Anything, everything could be wrong. But *what?* They are working on the problem she says. Jeanie's face and eyes betray her thoughts.

Craig has called from Charlotte several times. He says the problem must be with the machine. Inside I know my fear may be realized. Alone, I walk into 3109, as I walked into a room alone when Sandy was fourteen. And I set my Isaac on the altar and pray. *I gave my son to you before and he is still yours. I give him to you again.*

Suddenly, a great surge of peace and strength comes over me. I haven't asked for it, but I know it is there, and I know that in the next couple of hours I am going to need it. Calmly, I go back to the others, I touch Deb and hug Jeanie. The terrible anxiety that has built up all afternoon, though still there, now for a time is under control as we continue to wait.

At 6:50 the door opens. A doctor I have never seen before comes in. His face is solemn, so is his manner. He speaks quietly and deliberately. He is Dr. Sealy's associate. Dr. Sealy has asked him to come. They have finished the surgery, the problem has been corrected. But before our numbed minds can thaw to this good news, he goes on. There is another problem. They are trying various drugs and techniques, but they cannot get Sandy off the heart-lung machine. Suddenly the terrible truth hits me—his heart won't start!

Naive, innocent, or simply stunned, Deb asks, "What happens to people if they can't get them off the machine?"

The doctor looks at her, unprepared for the question. I put my arm around her. "Deb, if they can't get Sandy off the machine, he won't make it."

How long, I ask. An hour or an hour and a half. If it doesn't work in that time, there is no hope.

Oh, dear God! An anguished, silent cry from the depths is all Jeanie and I can manage. We have already prepared ourselves for this.

But Deb is pulling at her hair. "Oh, he can't die! God can't let him die! I will be so angry at God. Can't there be a transplant? I'll give him my heart!"

Now we tell everyone to prepare for the worst—Sandy has

problem; he may die. We gather and pray. More quickly than I can believe, people begin to arrive. Jeanie Spence is in the next room on her knees.

Irv calls Billy. Preston calls Kevin at Windy Gap and tells him only that the situation is very serious. Deb needs Craig terribly. I have him paged at Charlotte Memorial, tell him the problem and ask him to get someone to cover for him and come right up. We are whirling about in a maelstrom of calling, praying, crying and holding each other.

Sometime after 8:00 the door opens and Dr. Sealy and Dr. Gallagher come in. Dr. Sealy says what is needless to say, for we can read it in their faces: "We never got him off the table." We ask a few questions as to what happened and why.

Groping for control and understanding, Jeanie asks, "Has this ever happened before?"

"Yes, ma'am." But Dr. Sealy offers no more; there *is* nothing more to say.

I know we have to help these men. They are exhausted and in their own way are as devastated as we. I ask the doctors if we could pray. We had prayed with them before surgery. I thank God for his comfort, for the doctors, to be with them and to support us all in our grief. As they leave the room, I shake Dr. Sealy's hand and hug John Gallagher. He is absolutely stricken.

People begin to arrive, some with words of comfort, some overcome with tears and shaking. In the strength God has given me, I find myself trying to comfort others. One couple comes, cheerfully trying to see the good in the situation to glorify God. I wish they would simply cry with us.

Debbie Bowers comes with a letter to us from Sandy. He had written it the night before; we were to open it after surgery.

> Whatever happens I want you to know that I love you both immensely and hopefully the surgery is successful. . . . I know we have said that we have been retracing the steps of six years

ago but that is not really so. The Lord is reminding us of the great love among Christians and purifying us through suffering. It is not easy for me to realize these words even as I write them because I do not know whether my heart will be corrected or that I will wake up to unduly suffer. Thank you for your faithfulness to me and your love. Love, Sandy.

At this, we weep without restraint.

Now all we want is to go home. Irv and Preston have been handling the details, so there is little to do but sign a few papers, pack up Sandy's things and walk down a long corridor and out into the cold Carolina night.

When we stop for gas, I call Montreat to talk to Kevin. Billy has already brought him from Windy Gap. I tell him what happened and we cry a little. Through tears, questions and silence, we make our way home. It seems forever. Jeanie, her face sunken as if collapsing in upon itself, says, "Either God knows best or there is no God." It is just as stark a choice as that.

Finally, we are in Charlotte. Down familiar streets, dark and empty, we approach the house. The lights are on, cars are parked along the street. Friends are there with food and with hands to help carry things in. Craig has called. After I had called him, he drove all the way to Durham; we must have passed on the way In Durham, he had called Dr. Sealy and talked about the surgery He would be back around 1:30.

Deb cannot sleep by herself, so she crawls in with us. We lie there together and cry. After a while, Deb goes to her room and we sleep.

12
FINISHING
THE
RACE

*O*NE THING I DO, FORGETTING WHAT LIES BEHIND AND STRAINING forward to what lies ahead, I press on toward the goal for the prize of the upward call of God in Christ" (Phil 3:13-14).

"I have fought the good fight, I have run the race, I have kept the faith" (2 Tim 4:7).

Philippians 3:13-14 and 2 Timothy 4:7 both speak of striving to finish and if possible to win the race. These are the two passages most often cited by his friends when talking about Sandy. These passages comfort me for they suggest that it matters not how long your race—twenty-one years or eighty-one—but whether you run faithfully and finish. Paul felt he had. I trust God thinks Sandy did too since he seems to have destined him for twenty-one intense years—a sprint, not a distance run.

On the Friday night that Sandy died, sleep too was a welcome, though temporary, comfort, a numbed forgetting. But we awakened Saturday morning to a painful realization we could not bear alone. We awakened as if to darkness and not to light. Deb and Craig soon joined us; we lay in bed crying, trying somehow to comfort each other.

Before long, friends began to arrive. Some brought food; someone fixed the screen door, someone else raked the leaves we had neglected for ten traumatic days. Without the support of these friends, we would not have made it through funeral and burial arrangements, and the sheer numbing pain of Sandy's absence.

And through these early days too, we began for the first time to realize the extent of Sandy's impact on so many people. They called and wrote letters. They streamed through our house in a receiving line for nearly three hours the Sunday night after Sandy died. Some waited outside for half an hour or more in freezing weather. They testified at his memorial service. Later, Sandy was made a member of the Phi Beta Kappa honors society—the first, so we understood, to ever be admitted posthumously. These were a comfort to us too. Not that we wouldn't have given them up in an instant to have Sandy back! But because of Sandy's accomplishments, testimony and impact, ours was a clean grief. We had no painful regrets of the life he had lived; only a mournful longing for the life he might have lived.

Shortly before noon, Kevin arrived with his Uncle Billy. From my study, I saw them drive in, and went out and hugged Kevin. He stood there tall, grave, warm. We went for a long walk. He told me that when we called Windy Gap to tell him that Sandy's condition was "serious," he thought maybe it wasn't just serious, but a life-and-death situation. He went outside and cried and prayed for about forty-five minutes. During that time, he thought he heard Sandy say, "Good-by, Kevin." And he answered, "Good-by, Sandy. I love you."

"Uncle Billy told me you said something about climbing a mountain," I said. "What was that about?"

"When Uncle Billy came for me earlier than I'd expected, I figured Sandy must have died. So I asked him, how's Sandy? And he just told me it had been a long, hard surgery. When we got in the car, I asked him again, and he told me the Lord had taken Sandy home. Do you remember when we climbed Mount Debar together in New York just before Sandy went off to college? It was a hard climb and Sandy was usually ahead. Sometimes he would turn around and help me. Well in life, Dad, usually Sandy was ahead, but sometimes we helped each other too. But now Sandy has gotten to the top ahead of me, and there's no big rock to block his view—only beautiful paradise all around. He got there before us. Sandy was older and always beat me in everything. And just when I was beginning to catch up, he died. Now I'll never catch up or beat him in anything, Dad. But he has left me a standard to strive for for the rest of my life."

After the memorial service for Sandy in Chapel Hill, I went to his room in Granville West to pack up his things. On the wall was a poster showing a party of mountain climbers traversing the snowy shoulder of some mountain. Their footprints showed clearly in the snow behind them. The words on the poster read, "Where you are going is more important than where you have been."

On his desk I found an unfinished poem he had been working on, headed "To Dad, for his fiftieth birthday."

As the aged juice flows from the depth
    of the golden cup,
So your spirit of sweetness saturates those around.

Evident to all is your gentleness

like the laughing stream rolling over rocks
And softening them on a cool mountain evening.

And as the days go on, your wisdom is blossoming
    to the fullness
of the richness of the Appalachians.

What a golden honor it would be to don your mantle,
    to inherit twice times your spirit.
For then you would be me and I would continue to be you.

When I showed this poem to Norman Pell, our Australian crusade director, he was moved. "Leighton, I believe some of Sandy's spirit has been put in you." And indeed, this is what I have found. Because of his death, instead of my mantle falling on Sandy, his has fallen on me—and on many others.

I have become deeply convinced of the place of suffering and death in God's plan. When we plan our strategies for missions and evangelism—or any part of our life and work—we don't program an element of suffering. Nor should we, it would be morbid. There is no way we can plan for a young man's death, or his mother's grief-spawned eye spasms and lost weight, or his girlfriend's shattered dreams, or the loneliness of his mourning friends. Yet suffering is fertile ground for the gospel. The seed must fall into the ground and die.

But our slick, success-oriented plans for evangelism and ministry often ignore death and suffering. As Sandy said in his last letter to us, written the night before the operation, "I know we have said that we have been retracing the steps of six years ago. But that is not really so. The Lord is reminding us of the great love among Christians and purifying us through suffering." This purification may come through the death of our plans and programs, our ambitions, even the death of our noblest aspirations;

it may come even through the frustration of our greatest and most benign technical and scientific abilities.

Sandy's doctors suffered too, especially John Gallagher. He was very fond of Sandy. Both he and Dr. Sealy were personally and emotionally injured by Sandy's death; as world-class heart specialists, they were utterly stumped and defeated. They were doing the most advanced research in electrocardiology and surgical techniques. Gallagher thought they had controlled everything that could be controlled, had covered every variable. But the operation did not go as planned. They were able to sever the extra pathways in Sandy's heart, solving the WPW problem. But after working for hours, they were unable to get Sandy's heart to restart. At wit's end, Dr. Sealy asked if anyone had any suggestions. Terry Gullett, a nurse assigned to Sandy, suggested they pray; and she did.

When they lost Sandy, John was miserable. It was the worst experience of his life. "I learned I was not all-powerful; I could not do everything. I learned that when every variable has been covered, you still cannot control everything. You must always leave a part to God, fate, luck or whatever—call it what you like. Do what you can, then pray. We left too little to prayer, to what is not controllable. I never want to be that cocky again."

In John Gallagher's office, there is a photograph of our family. It hangs on the wall next to his desk at eye level. "Whenever I begin to feel cocky, I turn to the picture, say 'Hello, Sandy,' and I remember and am humbled."

The autopsy revealed something which left us all wondering about the dark and mysterious ways of God. As soon as Sandy's chest was open and his heart exposed, the doctors realized something more than WPW was wrong with Sandy's heart. It was not flexible as a healthy heart should be. It was tough, hard and slightly enlarged. The autopsy revealed that the walls of Sandy's heart had grown very thick. His heart was significantly heavier than the normal heart, but the extra, tough fibrous muscle was added *inside* the heart thus decreasing the volume of the heart's chambers. This condition is known as idiopathic concentric cardiomyopathy. As this condition continues, the volume of the chambers progressively diminishes until eventually the heart's capacity to pump blood is drastically reduced. Like bailing your boat with a teaspoon instead of a bucket. The surgery had corrected the WPW problem. But within a few years, very possibly, Sandy would have died or become a cardiac cripple, confined to a wheelchair because of the tiny capacity of his heart.

Who can understand these things? God seems to have programmed Sandy for twenty-one years. Something in Sandy seems to have sensed this and kept a faster, more intense pace for a shorter race. And during his short race, Sandy had reasons for confidence in the flesh—as did Paul. Both were used by God to influence others. But in Philippians, Paul considered all such accomplishments as rubbish. "If any other man thinks he has reason for confidence in the flesh, I have more. . . . But whatever gain I had, I counted as loss [rubbish]. . . . Because of the surpassing worth of knowing Christ Jesus my Lord" (Phil 3:4, 7-8). Moreover, even what he does desire, he has not yet fully attained. He presses on, but he has not yet arrived (Phil 3:12-14). Nor had Sandy arrived. He was no better nor any worse than Paul; his advantages in the flesh were rubbish in the face of his longing to know Christ, in the face of the overwhelming, unmerited grace of God.

Sandy was on the way, intensely striving, giving it his all. Yet, he was just on the way. How else are we to understand his contradictory mix of qualities—pride and humility, security and insecurity, legalism and grace—and our own? His was a mixed piety—like ours—but God used him mightily because, like David, he had a heart for God. He was giving God his best at every moment, regardless of how great or small that "best" was.

When Sandy was alive, he sometimes made his friends a little uncomfortable by being slightly apart, separate, present to the moment but not totally committed to this world, as if his eyes and mind were set on things above. Now that he is gone, his absence reminds us frequently of heaven, helping us to recover the old notion that our lives are brief, and lived continually under the eye of eternity and in the grace of God.

During the months following Sandy's death, to cope with my grief and sense of loss, I kept a journal. Through a series of "conversations" with Sandy, I continued to express my grief and bring our relationship to a close.

In one of those chats, I said, "Sandy, you've been dead two months earthtime."

"I feel as if I have been alive forever, Dad. It's a lot like one big long today."

"It's not a matter of time, Sandy, except that time heals. It's more a matter of nearness. I guess I'm concerned that as *our time* goes on, we will lose any sense of nearness."

"But why, Dad? You're moving closer to eternity every day. You're no longer moving from, but to me! And besides, the 'Wall' between is *so* thin—you would laugh if you could see it."

"I think more of you than when you were at Chapel Hill."

"Sure! I know you do. I hear those thoughts."

"Night, son! Enjoy the stars!"

"It's morning here, Dad. Enjoy the light!"

Pheidippides ran exhausted into Athens with news of the Greek victory at Marathon, shouting, "Rejoice! We conquer!" Sandy ran through the lives of those who knew him shouting, "Rejoice! He conquers!" Then, like the runner-warrior Pheidippides, he died.

Epilog

Time, they say, heals. Time also sets ambushes. On a cold, clear Carolina afternoon, driving by Myers Park High School, memories suddenly come flooding back.

I stop, park, walk around the track where he ran so many races. It's nearly seven years since Sandy ran his last race, over three years since he left us.

Passing the starting line, I wish he could start his whole life again. But would we want him back if it meant going through all the pain and hurt?

Suppose God had come to us and said, "You can have Sandy. Here is what he is going to be like, but you can have him for only twenty-one years!" What would we have chosen? No question. We would take him again—and again. But when you love deeply, you hurt deeply.

Nobody could have told me three years ago how much we would miss him or for how long. There is nothing quite like the death of a child. I guess most folks think that in a few weeks or in a few months the pain is over. Maybe for some people. But not for me. Not for Jeanie.

I want so much to see him again. Watch his flying feet going around the track. See him duck his head in a moment of embarrassment. Watch him touch the corner between his eyes and his nose when he is thinking. See him pray, legs apart, long fingers pressing together, moving them up and down or pulling them apart when he can't get the right word. But the pain of death is its finality. Things are never the same again.

And yet they have gotten better. We can talk more freely about Sandy now. As a family we can laugh at his foibles, remembering how spacey he could be. But still I find it hard to look at his picture. Deb can't read his journals. Jeanie's eyelids began having spasms three months after he died. They are better but still not perfect. And still the questions come.

I walk around the final curve on the track, past the green wall with the sign, "Go Mustangs," past the scoreboard. I stop and look down at the spot twenty yards from the finish line where his legs began to wobble in that final race.

Why? What happened that day? Why did his heart run away again? Why did the doctors say he could run? Why did we let him run? Why was his heart flawed in the first place? Was it the German measles that Jeanie was exposed to when she was carrying Sandy that did it? And why was he not healed?

So many questions. So few answers. "Where is God, Mom?" Sandy said, during his last illness. "I don't feel him. I need to feel him." And we have felt the same thing.

When I prayed the day before his surgery I said, "God, be good to my boy." But he died. Was God good to him?

When we get down to it, I guess Jeanie put it right that last night, "Either there is a God and he is good, or there is no God."

Atheists might not have such a big problem. They could shrug off such events as fate. So life is meaningless and why does it matter how long anyone lives? It is all an accident anyway. And in that case, why do I love? Chemicals, loving chemicals.

How absurd!

But we did love him. And we do. And life is not nothing. So we choose to dwell, not on the pain of losing him, but on the wonder that we had him at all.

"When a good young man dies; what a waste, who can explain it?" That question headlined a newspaper story the Sunday after Sandy died. Many would say, "What a tragedy; his race was cut short." But that gives me pause. Is *tragic* a word that belongs in a Christian's vocabulary? Pain and suffering, yes, and loss and anguish and questioning. But *tragedy* is a word from the ancient Greeks not from the language of the Bible.

I have looked at a lot of Sandy's pictures since he died. And I have realized what a very great difference it makes whether I look at them from the viewpoint of life or of death.

Here is what I mean. When Sandy was physically alive and with us I would have looked at those pictures with more or less interest, regret or pride, with a sense of wonder at what he grew into.

Now, after his death, I look at each one with a little voice saying over my shoulder, "How tragic, that Sandy would only live until he was twenty-one."

It is the same way when I read his journal. I tend to read with a tragic sense that keeps murmuring, "And he only had six months, or one month, or one week to live."

How important then to decide what is Sandy's true end! If twenty-one years *was* the end, then it does seem tragic. (Then I must discover why it is tragic and not a meaningless event to be shrugged off. If there is nothing *more,* then there really is *nothing*—nothing ultimately important.)

But if eternity is his end, then I can look from his infancy to his manhood and see each part fitting into an eternal whole which is yet beyond my ken, but not my hope.

On the one view, death leads to the trash heap.

On the other, death is swallowed up in glory.

So as I think of the infant son who became our grown-up son, I can imagine him a man who has become a glorious creature of eternity.

Philosophizing though does not take away the pain that twists my insides when I think how achingly I miss him. But as Jeanie has reminded me, "We have got to see things from Sandy's perspective."

Was twenty-one years enough? Or would twenty-two have been enough? Or twenty-three? Or would it have taken seventy-three? Then why not seventy-four?

Isn't it what fills those years that matters? Is time just clock-time or opportunity-time—or God-time? Is it how long or how full? For Sandy, the cup of time was running over. God so filled those years that they are going to keep brimming over.

Right here somewhere along this track, he learned to pass the baton on to his teammates. He did it in life, he did it in death. I think of so many who have picked up the baton and have run on—Fran, Susan, Billy, Lisa, Kendall, Kevin.

The year after Sandy died, Kevin and I were raking leaves and talking about how we missed him. Kevin said, "But, Dad, maybe Sandy's influence has been far greater than if he had lived. His life was like a very bright light—a spotlight—focused intensely. But his death has been a floodlight. It has covered a much wider area."

Again, I have become convinced that John 12 is not just a metaphor but a literal truth. "Unless a grain of wheat falls into the ground and dies, it abides alone, but if it dies it brings forth many seeds."

Life blossoming from death. That is God's way. It is the way of the cross. And we have seen how God has taken characteristics of Sandy, godly traits, and placed them into the friends who loved him. More compassion into one. More commitment into another.

But not everybody has picked up the baton. Some of his friends have let it fall. Or took it and then stepped aside. "Is this what you get for following Christ—for pursuing God—to die young?" I can imagine some of them saying that.

"But what are the options?" I want to ask. "To be bad and die young? To be bad and die old? Or to be neutral and count for nothing?"

I guess what we would all like is to be good and have fun and die old. I wish with all my heart that could have been for Sandy. But it wasn't to be.

We have no regrets. No unsaid words we wished we had said. No desire that Sandy had been a different kind of person. At least, as someone said, Jeanie and I have "clean sorrow." Still, I want him. I want to see those pounding feet, the curly hair, the smile, the serious, thoughtful eyes. I want him to run not just here on the track but all through his life.

Yes, I believe God is good and strong and that he brings blessing out of pain. But I would be less than honest if I didn't acknowledge the part of me inside that says, "It is not right."

It is not right that Sandy is not coming home again. It is not right that he doesn't share the joys and triumphs of his brother's life, and of his sister's little son, Graham, who will only know Uncle Sandy by his picture. It is not right that he will not marry and have children. It is not right that he is not going to fulfill the ministry that we believe might have been there.

I sense these things inside myself and I ask, "Am I doubting God?"

But Sandy's death is *not* right. As Christians we sometimes too easily and glibly pass over things that happen with nice sweet words, and forget that it is not right.

I remember that our Lord stood at the grave of his friend,

Lazarus. The Scripture says that he was "deeply troubled in his spirit" (Jn 11:33). The word taken literally means he "snorted" in his spirit like a warhorse facing battle, seeing what death and evil had done to the beautiful world his Father had made. And for a beautiful young man, it is not right.

We can't just gloss that over. I think that's what Paul meant in 1 Corinthians 15, when he stated "the last enemy to be destroyed is death." Death is an enemy. The gospel is not a sugar coating to make a bitter pill taste better. The gospel is the difference between life and death. If Christ has not been raised, our faith is vain, and those who have died are gone forever. If only for this life we have hope in Christ, we are to be pitied. But Christ indeed has been raised from the dead and has become the firstfruits of those who have fallen asleep (1 Cor 15:16-20).

Weeks after Sandy died, a letter came from the missionary under whose direction he worked that summer in France. He wrote, "We are so earthbound. We assume that the main part of God's will and work is here on earth. I believe that not only the best is yet to come, but the highest will also be there . . . *God never wastes anything* . . . rather than being the end, this is the Beginning!"

So I stand here on the track. With my toe, I draw a line where the finish line was, where Sandy finished his last race. But the finish line is also the starting line. And that is what makes the pain bearable. That is what undergirds the loss with hope. That is what makes the race worth running. Suppose that life is not the race. Suppose life is only the training season, and Eternity is the real race.

Then Sandy's heart was beating, not just for a medley relay, not just twenty-one years, but for eternity. The weight he carried—including a wounded heart—was preparing him for an eternal weight of glory.

Sometimes in my mind, I whisper, "What is it like, son?"

And I hear him say, "I can think so deeply and every thought is clear. I can speak and express exactly what I mean. I can run and never get tired. I am so surefooted in the paths of glory."

So a son leaves a legacy for a father. I have determined to run my race for Christ to the end. And when that time comes maybe our Savior will let him come running to meet me. Then with all sons and daughters of the resurrection, our hearts will beat and run for God forever.

Sandy Ford Memorial Fund

The Leighton Frederick Sandys Ford, Jr., Scholarship Memorial Fund was begun immediately after Sandy's death to help other young people to prepare for specific careers in evangelism or missions. In this way they are carrying on the race for Christ which Sandy has completed.

The response to the Fund has been widespread and substantial scholarship help has been available. Recipients are carefully chosen by a selection committee on the basis of having demonstrated outstanding leadership and spiritual maturity.

Each year the number of applicants increases. The vision is that the Fund will grow until hundreds of young people can be helped to invest their lives in the service of Christ. Readers who have been moved by the story of Sandy and who are interested in contributing to the Fund or learning more about it may write to:

The Leighton Frederick Sandys Ford, Jr., Memorial Fund,
c/o Billy Graham Evangelistic Association Ltd,
27 Camden Road, London NW1 9LN, England.

GLOSSARY

Alexander Graham
Sandy's high school in Charlotte, North Carolina.

all-quad meeting
A meeting of all four chapters, or Christian Unions, of the large University of North Carolina.

blueberry bread
A bread made of blueberries (bilberries), in the manner of banana cake.

chapter of Inter-Varsity
A Christian Union linked to the Inter-Varsity Christian Fellowship, the US equivalent of the Universities and Colleges Christian Fellowship.

Chapel Hill
The location of the University of North Carolina.

class of 1979
I.e. graduation class of that particular year.

EKG
ECG, or electrocardiogram.

elective
Course option.

fraternity
Men's student society (see also *sorority*).

frat house
See 'fraternity'. This is a student house occupied by members of
a particular fraternity.

freshman
Fresher, or first-year student.

'go-fer' boy
An allusion to slavery. The slave had to go for this or that on his
master's (Massa's) orders.

to goof off
To mess around.

graduate
Postgraduate. It can also refer to a graduate of high school.

handoff
The passing of the baton in a relay race.

intern
An assistant's or an interim job for a recent graduate or advanced student.

Inter-Varsity Christian Fellowship
This is an evangelical student movement active in hundreds of universities, colleges and schools of nursing in the United States. It is a member movement of the International Fellowship of Evangelical Students and its equivalent in the British Isles is the Universities and Colleges Christian Fellowship.

jiving
Chatting.

a jock
A very athletic person.

junior high
Secondary school to around the age of fourteen.

junior year
The third of the four-year university course.

major
The major field of one's university study.

paramedic
Name of emergency medical support staff.

Phi Beta Kappa honor society
A fraternity. Only students with a first-class grade point average would be invited to join this highly élite society.

Phi Eta Sigma honor society
Only students with a first-class grade point average would be invited to join this élite society.

pledge
If a student is accepted into a fraternity or sorority he or she becomes a 'pledge', and often has to go through initiation rites.

PJs
Pyjamas.

professor
A university lecturer.

program chairman of Inter-Varsity
The person responsible for devising the programme of the Christian Union.

school
An educational establishment, including university or college.

semester
In the USA, the academic year is divided into halves, called semesters.

seminary
An institution for postgraduate theological study.

senior high
The final stage of secondary school (usually for 14–18 years of age).

senior year
The final year of the four-year university course.

sophomore
A second-year university or high school student.

sorority
The female equivalent of a fraternity, a women's society in university or college.

spacey
In another world; on another wavelength; in a world of one's own.

state school
A state university. Fees are cheaper for those attending the university of their state. The University of North Carolina, which Sandy attended, is a state university.

strep (throat)
An abbreviation of *streptococcus*. A severe sore throat.

student government
High school students take this very seriously. Members are elected by their peers, and are involved in such things as programmes for graduation ceremonies, and school policy.

track
Running. Cross-country running, for example, is called 'cross-country track'.

tubing
This refers to floating on a river by primitive means such as a raft or an inner tube from a tyre.

UNC
The University of North Carolina, which Sandy attended.

Urbana
A large triennial student missionary conference in North America.

wieners
Frankfurters, or hot dogs.

WPW
The Wolfe-Parkinson-White syndrome, Sandy's heart defect (see pages 28, 29).